Some Styles of Masculinity

Some Styles of Masculinity

Gregg Bordowitz

Introduction by Hua Hsu

Triple Canopy

Some Styles of Masculinity

Edited by Alexander Provan and Maya Binyam
Published by Triple Canopy, New York, 2021

Some Styles of Masculinity is adapted from the eponymous series of monologues, which was commissioned by the New Museum and presented in 2018 as part of the exhibition "Trigger: Gender as a Tool and a Weapon." The monologues have subsequently been presented by the Douglas F. Cooley Memorial Art Gallery at Reed College (Portland); the Art Institute of Chicago; and MoMA PS1 (New York City). *Some Styles of Masculinity* also incorporates material from *Only Idiots Smile* (2017), a video created by Bordowitz in conjunction with the monologues and exhibited at "Trigger"; *Answers with Questions* (2020), a three-episode advice show hosted by Bordowitz and produced and published by Triple Canopy; and *Gimme Danger* (2018), a performance by Bordowitz that was commissioned and presented by Triple Canopy.

ISBN 978-0-9978524-5-5

Printed by Shapco Printing
Minneapolis, MN, USA

Triple Canopy
264 Canal Street, 3W
New York, NY 10013
canopycanopycanopy.com
Triple Canopy is a nonprofit
501(c)(3) organization

This book is dedicated to Lauren Berlant (1957–2021), z”l. Lauren was the first person to write about my work and to recognize it for what it is: art made by a depressed and angry person. Lauren mapped the affective terrain of my videos, writing, and performances. *Some Styles of Masculinity* is completely indebted to Lauren’s work, especially their writing on humor (and humorlessness).

—*Gregg Bordowitz*

Preface

On three successive nights in January 2018, Gregg Bordowitz sauntered onto a stage in a museum basement, squinted as he surveyed the audience of friends and strangers, and introduced himself as Benyamin Zev. He'd been billed as presenting a trio of lectures, but there was no podium set up, no slide show on screen. Behind him, attached to a curtained wall, was a hand-painted sign with the silhouette of a howling wolf encircled by THE BENYAMIN ZEV SHOW. Bordowitz, wearing a black suit and black tie, looked the part of a family-friendly 1960s talk-show host, though the oversized, gold-encased ruby on his finger seemed to belong to an immortal mystic or glam icon. He gripped a microphone, his ring glinting under the stage lights, and began not with a thesis but a reflection on his own names, Gregg and Benyamin: American and Jewish, artifacts of twentieth-century assimilation and age-old custom, sources of alienation and belonging. Then he launched into a freewheeling monologue on being different when difference is under assault, and inhabiting multiple names, voices, and identities.

Each of Bordowitz's nightly monologues addressed a totem of masculinity: the rock star, rabbi, and comedian. Growing up as a Yinglish-speaking

Jew in Queens in the 1970s, these figures enabled Bordowitz to imagine himself as something besides an upwardly mobile professional—doctor, lawyer, financier—or an outer-borough relic. From the gender-bending, genre-defying act of Lou Reed, the radical, searching theology of Abraham Joshua Heschel, and the irreverent, roving improvisations of Lenny Bruce, Bordowitz learned how to balance tradition and reinvention, and how to use history to form the future. The rock star, rabbi, and comedian spoke to the vexing choice facing people like him: be different or become American, remain on the margins of society or go along with the constant reinforcement of whiteness. These unlikely avatars of masculinity also prepared him for life as a queer person, offering models of performance, pleasure, faith, reflection, and resistance.

After debuting *Some Styles of Masculinity* at the New Museum in New York City, Bordowitz reprised the performances for exhibitions at the Art Institute of Chicago, Reed College's Cooley Gallery, and MoMA PS1. The sets shifted, but the props remained much the same: an ad hoc library of formative books on the subjects at hand, accoutrements of Jewish worship, and a playlist stocked with punk rock and klezmer. Bordowitz improvised as he spoke to the audience, shuttling between practiced anecdotes, stream-of-consciousness commentaries, anachronistic Jewish jokes, and agonizing accounts of the (ongoing) AIDS crisis, which has preoccupied him since he tested positive for HIV and became a core member of the AIDS Coalition to Unleash Power (ACT UP) in the late 1980s. He punctuated the monologues with songs from his playlist, which transported the audience to the moments in which he'd heard them, bridging present and past, listener and speaker. He got laughs, then wondered why the audience was laughing—and whether Americans had been lulled into believing that they'd get through the white supremacism and fascism of the Trump administration by chuckling at late-night shows.

From the moment we saw Bordowitz on stage, we knew that we wanted to transform *Some Styles of Masculinity* into a book. We weren't interested in a faithful record of the monologues, since reproducing the experience of being in the room—and of Bordowitz essaying in real time, responding to the audience and the moment—seemed preposterous. Instead, we wanted to produce a comparable effect in print, with the page and reader substituting for the stage and audience. We wanted to translate Bordowitz's looseness and liveness into writing, while expanding the monologues to encompass not only the hour of the performances but the following months and years. And we wanted to maintain the sense of Bordowitz as the embodiment of his own argument: that identity is a continual process of asking questions in the company of friends and strangers.

After conferring with Bordowitz—who steers clear of documentation of his performances—we pored over transcripts from several iterations of the monologues. We edited, expanded, and embellished them until we had three chapters, each presenting a monologue that seems to have occurred on a single night but is, in fact, a composite. We made use of the conventions of documentation in order to mark crucial moments on and off stage—dancing, coughing, interrupting, laughing—and to occasionally situate the reader between the event and page, between then and now. Rather than ask Bordowitz to overwrite the record of himself performing, we instigated monologues on Zoom and in the park, asking him questions and integrating his responses. Our conversations reflected all that had changed and remained the same since 2017, when Bordowitz was inspired by the Charlottesville white-nationalist rally to "take my Jewish act on the road, *schmear* myself in *schmaltz*, and grease up the fucking world." Inevitably, we came to understand the monologues in relation to the present—the pandemic years of 2020 and 2021, marked by the menace of fascism and the promise of uprising—and we shaped them accordingly, with the intent to furnish these pages with ample grease for the future.

—Alexander Provan and Maya Binyam

Introduction by Hua Hsu

1.

When I was growing up I rarely thought about masculinity, which is one of the main privileges it affords. Back then, in the 1980s and '90s, so long as you weren't bad in some crass, pawing, physically aggressive way, you could consider yourself good. But the gradient of masculine identities seemed so basic and finite—from jock to nerd—that, to me, the only real option was to reject all of them, to embrace the absence of viable models. As a young Asian American, I thought of this as a natural response, given how many provinces of masculinity seemed to be permanently off limits. I could never imagine myself as a leading man or star athlete, and I remember feeling liberated when I accepted that as the case: my alternative to being brutish and gross was none of the above.

Yet even the rejection of masculinity is about following scripts. Negating whatever everyone else affirmed meant that I'd at least skimmed my lines. I knew what was expected of me. Perhaps discouraging myself from interrogating the process—and eventual product—of becoming a man was as much a script as all the buffoonish stuff, the locker room roughhousing and unashamed ogling. I didn't realize as a teenager that identities are false horizons, projects that are undertaken but never truly finished. The nature of the performance changes with the times, with the person.

Now I know that you write sentences over and over until your penmanship improves, and you learn to fit in by repeating the gestures deemed normal, or normal enough. But you're always passing; you're always covering for someone else's discomfort, answering to a name that sounds close enough to your own. You hold a shirt up to your chest and imagine how you'll be received. You clear your throat even when nobody is around.

More than ever, you go through these motions in public, whether the public is real or imagined, physical or online. Every facet of personal identity authorizes some new skirmish in the forever culture war, and few fault lines are as fraught as masculinity. Some say the problem with this country is that we need to be manly again: straight-shooter demagogues decry liberal softness, men's rights activists dwell on their own victimhood, and tech utopians consult the noble caveman for diet advice. Others point out that masculinity, predatory and unfeeling, is the cause of our problems, not the solution to them. The adjective they're most likely to modify "masculinity" with is "toxic." A distant second might be "new," which vaguely names the remedy. To me, the attempts to tout a new—more thoughtful, historically distinct—form of masculinity feel a bit superficial, as if outfitting movie stars and rappers in designer kilts could put a dent in centuries of egomaniacal conquest and domination. Or maybe the new masculinity just feels like ad copy, devised to open our minds to updated fabrics and silhouettes.

How else have the times changed? I think of "The American Male at Age Ten," the essay Susan Orlean wrote three decades ago that probes the perspective of a fifth-grade New Jerseyite and imagines what he'll be like as a man. At the time, she could publish a charming and innocent story about a typical boy brought up in "a town of amazing lawns" and make light of his amorphous, prepubescent destructiveness—after all, he was just a kid. She could conclude: "The collision in his mind of what he understands, what he hears, what he figures out, what popular culture pours into him, what he knows, what he pretends to know, and what he imagines, makes an interesting mess." But we're more enlightened these days; we know that a typical boy is trouble (and is *in* trouble).

2.

One of the stranger aspects of the 2017 Unite the Right rally in Charlottesville was the preponderance of khaki. Browsing the images of protesters in the hours leading up to the violence, which left three dead and dozens injured, I expected to see outdoorsy types cavorting in tactical gear. Instead, I saw photo after photo of young white men wearing crisp polo shirts and khaki pants. In isolation, any one of them looked boring: a nonthreatening conformist. But in the photos showing hundreds of marchers illuminated by torches, the costume took on a different meaning. Crisis had gripped our most generic men.

In the following hours, I watched the show of uniformity shift to violence, and I wondered what the scenes said about contemporary manhood and masculinity. What were the remaining alternatives to the standard scripts? What version of conformity was drawing these angry young men, many of whom brandished anti-Semitic signs? Do all attempts at cultural assimilation simply uphold the nation's white-supremacist core, whether the upwardly mobile outsiders are Asian American or Jewish?

As I was clicking on the updates, Gregg Bordowitz was loading images of the same signs and asking himself the same questions. He searched for "Jews will not replace us," and he resolved to meet the charge of engineering a minority takeover by performing his ethnicity on stage, by taking his "queer, communist, Jewish ass on the road." He began interrogating the influences that had shaped him, reflecting on his teenage years, which he'd spent constantly attending to the question of what kind of man he might become: queer or straight, Jewish or American, punk or poser. All of the paths leading to the generic, normative male had required him—a bookish, outer-borough son of working-class parents—to deny a fundamental part of himself. Eventually, though, he figured out how to become something else, assembling a model of masculinity that hinged on three personas that he had admired and studied: the rock star, the rabbi, and the comedian.

Several months after Charlottesville, as part of an exhibition at the New Museum, Bordowitz debuted *Some Styles of Masculinity*, a trio of improvised monologues on these figures and how they'd shaped him, how they'd enabled him to go off script and to cultivate a performance of gender that accounted for his particular understanding of race, ethnicity, and nationality.[1] The monologues are sincere and hopeful, weird and campy. Bordowitz, who was born in 1964, returns to his roots: he performs under his

1 The versions of the monologues in this book are adapted from transcripts of multiple performances in 2018 and 2019, and incorporate material from related works as well as conversations between Bordowitz and the editors. Though each chapter purports to present a single monologue that took place on a particular evening, the book serves to distill, revise, and reinvent Bordowitz's improvisations for the page, rather than document events.

Hebrew name, Benyamin Zev, fulfilling his longtime fantasy of hosting a variety show. He regards his own body—the way he speaks, stands, listens—as he describes how he became who he is: through worshiping Lou Reed, studying Lenny Bruce routines, absorbing Jewish liberation theology, and engaging in the confrontational, in-the-streets action of late-eighties AIDS activism. But he acts less like a pedagogue or narrator than the host of an off-kilter, otherworldly take on *The Carol Burnett Show* or *The Dick Van Dyke Show*. He addresses the audience, casting about for reactions, but he also looks past the crowd—and past the reader—for an audience that has yet to assemble.

3.

When I first read *Some Styles of Masculinity*, I approached Bordowitz's monologues ethnographically, as a chance to learn about someone else's life and experience of being a man. After all, I can't remember ever seeing a variety show or listening to Barbra Streisand. Generally, I don't read anything expecting to see myself—a vestige of my conditioning. I'm always showing up to learn about the proverbial other, and Bordowitz counts: he's an artist and activist who's been living with HIV for more than half of his life, and he's been devoted to chronicling the AIDS pandemic while organizing against the forces that have perpetuated the suffering. Here are some other obvious and important ways in which he and I are different: He was born in Brooklyn in 1964, his lineage consisting of "poor Jews from undistinguished European shtetls" who came through Ellis Island. I was born in Champaign–Urbana, Illinois, in 1977, to graduate students who'd immigrated from Taiwan. He has a Hebrew name and even a middle name (a sign of trading Jewish tradition for the aspiration to assimilate); I have neither. He is a proper, lifelong New Yorker, with stories about the downtown scene of the 1980s and harassing Allen Ginsberg; I came of age in the suburbs of Silicon Valley, with stories about my dad's anonymous engineer friends. He is a queer Jewish man who sees no contradiction between faith and queerness; in fact, he credits his reading of scripture for his commitment to liberation. I didn't grow up with faith in any discernible way, and I had to look up "shtetl" and "Talmud."

In the monologues, Bordowitz, as Benyamin Zev, unthreads himself. He delves into the meaning of names—his names, the names of God, the names assumed by punk rock icons to conceal their Jewish roots—as signs of tradition and reinvention, nation and diaspora. He lingers on how the weighty matters that are to be taken seriously—the nature of divinity, the tenuous assimilation of Jews and other ethnic groups in order to maintain the hegemony of whiteness, the blood on the hands of the Centers for Disease Control—and the trivial phenomena that are to be bracketed as entertainment—*Seinfeld*, Streisand, Yiddish humor, disco music—converge in the formation of taste and how, in turn, taste becomes a marker of identity. In relaying how he became himself through the media he consumed and the personas he encountered, Bordowitz recovers a distinctly twentieth-century relationship to the world, which, to me, has to do with being held at arm's length from the culture. We weren't all viral-stars-in-waiting. We didn't yet have the tools to broadcast ourselves and our art into the world on a minute-by-minute basis. Taste was as much an expression of resourcefulness as of discernment.

As Bordowitz observes in his monologues—and demonstrates on stage—masculinity finds expression in how people hold their bodies and present their faces, but also in language, in the exploration of texts. And that exploration is about sorting through relationships that may or may not exist: building a world—or gleaning the possibility of a different world—from the lyrics of a rock song, the commentary of a medieval rabbi, and the transmission of a Jewish joke. Bordowitz figures himself out in real time, drawing on philosophical lineages and artistic legacies that speak to me but also make me feel like an outsider, a visitor to someone else's home. Yet there's something across the chasm of times and bodies that I find irresistible about the act of monologuing, about Bordowitz's digressions and riffs, which intersect and accumulate until they resemble the arc of a life. I'm familiar with the drive and reluctance to assimilate; I catch echoes of my own interactions and fixations, my own desire for new affiliations and accidental solidarities, my own draft of a narrative.

Reading *Some Styles of Masculinity* is like spying my reflection in someone else's mirror, from the deliberate choice of cool alienation over superficial belonging to the temporary solace found in rejecting the world that seems to have rejected you. "What else can you do if you've got no time, no future?" Bordowitz asks, synthesizing Lou Reed and the Sex Pistols. "One thing you can do, I suppose, is retreat from the world—or create a world apart from the one that's defined you as a loser, an outsider, a threat, a reprobate, a vector of disease." Despite the decade between me and Bordowitz, I recall the compulsion to immerse myself in small effects, the desire to see how much I could do—and what I could make of myself—with extremely limited resources. *Some Styles of Masculinity* sends me back to a time when the radio represented "freedom" and "mobility," when I was so entranced by a new song that nothing else mattered—certainly not the constraints of where I found myself, in the suburbs of the South Bay. I remember bouncing "between feeling rooted and feeling displaced, between getting away from something and moving toward something." Any zine I came across provided a blueprint for a new identity. Whatever indie LPs were for sale at my local record shop became my favorites, since they were the only ones I could listen to (and so I listened to them over and over again). Instead of a culture scaffolded by algorithms, I had chance and randomness.

For Bordowitz, encountering rock stars, rabbis, and comedians provided rare models for assimilation *and* resistance. "Music gave me a sense of my masculinity—a claim to my masculinity," he says. "And music showed me the possibilities of expression: how to rebel or conform, how to be myself or become someone else." Studying the cover of Lou Reed's *Transformer*, which features the former Velvet Underground frontman in mascara on the front and a femme fatale lookalike on the back, compelled Bordowitz to form "an idea of masculinity that merged Jewishness with queerness." Idolizing rock stars like Reed—the only god he needed—trained Bordowitz to be a man, the sort of man he hadn't been able to envision on his own. "I imagined a world based on those pictures," he explains, referring to *Transformer*, "and a role for me in that world."

Actually, Bordowitz's models of masculinity may have shown him how to destroy worlds as much as how to compose himself. Listening to songs like the Dictators' "Master Race Rock" and the Ramones' "Blitzkrieg Bop"—and witnessing (Jewish) punk's dalliance with Nazi iconography—made him *feel* contradictions that he hadn't previously known how to describe. Still, today, listening to these songs with Bordowitz is to get a lesson not only in pissing off Jewish parents but in demolishing the boundaries that shape who we are—our values, our sense of obligation to history, and our notions of how to dress and behave. On one hand, Bordowitz is intrigued by the Jewishness of the artists whose personas and performances he parses: the Ramones and other bands of outer-borough punks who rejected the path to assimilation, turning stigma into a badge of honor; Lenny Bruce and the "sick comedians," whose biting, audacious routines were steeped in the "anger, resentment, and alienation" of immigrant households; and the Barry Sisters, whose "Yiddish swing" could only have been made in America, as Jews tried to figure out where they fit into a Black and white world. On the other hand, Bordowitz notes that heritage was never so fixed as to force a choice between conformity and abandonment, which he proves by reading sacred texts and canonical songs against the grain. Recalling a world of finite possibilities, he listens to and reads the same things over and over until they make up a story that is altogether different from the ones he'd previously been told. The Talmud is not simply the hallowed sourcebook of Jewish theology but a kind of technology: a means of transmission made possible by—and sustaining—the diaspora; "the radio before the radio," hailing the past and future in the present.

4.

"I want you to feel like I do, like you're trapped inside my head," Bordowitz says. How does it feel to constantly unmake and remake yourself as you shuttle between klezmer and house music, the history of fascism and the late-night comics lampooning Trump, the question of divine intervention and the negligence of the federal government in the face of a pandemic? How does it feel to be inside Bordowitz's head? Overwhelming, almost suffocating: the incessant firing of associations, with memories triggering songs, songs triggering theological discourses, discourses triggering jokes, jokes triggering polemics, and on and on. A meditation on diaspora as a state of being (and not a right to a preordained homeland) links the great theorist Stuart Hall to the question of God's agency in the world to the inheritance of Jewish culture (and formation of Jewish subcultures), all of which connect to the casual drift of radio waves. "If you've got no homeland to return to, you have to figure out another path," Bordowitz says, thinking of himself in terms of the circulation of people and information through space and time. He has become the radio.

As Bordowitz talks, he leads us further away from some imagined home, further into the wilderness. And that's the point: he's asking questions rather than providing answers, much less selling a template or pattern of thought to eager consumers. Feeling like Bordowitz isn't at all the same as identifying with him. As I began to read *Some Styles of Masculinity*—as I wandered into the trap—I worried not only about missing references but failing to make much of the figures that have been so meaningful to Bordowitz. I'd come across Desmond Dekker, the Ramones, Lenny Bruce, Lou Reed, and Iggy Pop as vintage culture, markers of cool that had been vetted and passed down to me; I didn't have to discern their value on the fly, and I couldn't do anything with them that was particular to me (i.e., that hundreds of thousands of alienated youths hadn't already done). Many of Bordowitz's totems are not mine, I realized, and many of mine may be junk to him. In some cases, though, they're the same, and they're shared by countless others, yet each of us thinks he has a distinct, even singular relationship with them. Nevertheless, I found myself deferring to Bordowitz as I read: he understands a singer's expression of anguish—the combination of a lyric, sneer, and outfit—in a way that none of the rest of us do. At first, like so many others, he sees Iggy Pop or Lou Reed and he's excited, troubled, disoriented. Then, one day, he's intuited an entire worldview from the way a singer's hair feathers in the middle.

Despite the tragedy and loss that he's witnessed, Bordowitz doesn't look backwards in order to assign blame or settle scores. He isn't rooting around for the origins of toxic masculinity; he isn't fixating on the bullies who called him names, mocked his speech, and heckled him at protests. He doesn't fault others for his alienation, and he doesn't chastise the generations of immigrants that, like my family, assimilated into suburban cul-de-sacs. Rather than vie to be normal, Bordowitz recognizes the possibility of making a good life by addressing your own, whatever that means; by constituting communities that are intimate and small; by seeking out the margins, where people implicitly understand one another. He appreciates the Borscht Belt comedians who told corny one-liners to post-buffet crowds, even as he sides with Lenny Bruce and Johnny Thunders, even as he comes to see the divide between the mainstream and the counterculture as mostly unbridgeable, despite the sporadic flickers of a radio signal passing information between the spheres.

Occasionally, Bordowitz fondly recalls his former selves: the adolescent poser and fraud, the defiant maverick who refused community for fear of being categorized and becoming static. Many of us would rather forget the petulance of our younger days, but Bordowitz embraces the rough drafts of himself as an artist and activist and reminds us that, if we're lucky, the drafts keep coming. These are versions of Bordowitz that failed as men, but ultimately won. They're anticipations of futures that never arrived, but survive in fragments. They're manifestations of styles that can still be worn, and that can always be worn differently. By treating them as such, Bordowitz opens up a range of paths and evolutions to come, and he, too, plays an archetype: the omnivorous enthusiast, the obsessive critic, the swooning fan. He makes room for you, the reader, to channel your inner Benyamin Zev. *Some Styles of Masculinity* is a set of monologues as well as an invitation to contemplate your own performance, imagine your own show, and construct the world in which that show airs before a live audience chanting all of your names.

Chapter 1: The Rock Star

I'm Gregg Bordowitz. Gregg David Bordowitz, actually. Why the two g's? So that no one calls me Gregory. And because I'm American: picture me in Greenwich, wearing pink shorts, sipping a gin and tonic, watching my compatriots volley on a grass court.

My middle name is another mark of patriotism. Jews don't usually have middle names. Does anyone know where middle names come from? The Middle Ages. Europeans came up with baptismal names so they didn't have to choose between naming kids after family members or saints. Eventually, most of them abandoned the saints and went with names such as ... David. When families like mine—poor Jews from undistinguished European shtetls—arrived at Ellis Island, we followed suit. You know, a middle name is the first step on the social ladder.

I've always been interested in names—G-d's name, especially, but also my own. It's not quite as rich as a topic, but it's easier to pronounce. There's no taboo on saying "Gregg."

When I was born, I was named Gregg Harstein. Harstein is the name of my biological father, who left us when I was four. All I knew about him was that he was a musician and he did drugs. He wasn't very happy being married and having a kid, so he and my mom made a deal: he gave me up for adoption so that I could take my stepfather's name, Bordowitz, and he waived his visitation rights; my mother, in exchange, let him get away with not paying alimony—or paying for anything else.

[*Pauses for two seconds; squints at the stage lights while scanning the audience.*]

Not a laugh in the house? No—not funny.

Don't worry, my mom wasn't swindled; she knew he'd never send us a dime, so she decided to free herself from ever expecting anything from him. And she managed. Her name, I think, is fitting: Linda Bonnie Bordowitz. Her maiden name was Glassman—maker of transparent and fragile vessels, whether from sand or flesh—but her Hebrew name was Leah Binah. Leah is a biblical name—Jacob's first wife—that means "weary." And Binah is the Hebrew word for understanding, or wisdom. That makes my mother "weary wisdom."

Who am I? Tonight, I'm trading Gregg Bordowitz for my Hebrew name, Benyamin Zev. I, Benyamin Zev, always wanted to do a variety show. I grew up watching *The Carol Burnett Show* and, finally, four decades later, I've got *Some Styles of Masculinity*.

And I've got you all to complete my fantasy. I hope you're pleased; I hope the format is as fresh today as in 1974.

I wanted the set to have a wandering-Jew-unpacking-his-library feel.

[*Points to the books and other objects on shelves on the stage.*]

These beloved books constitute my research for the show—and, I suppose, they constitute myself: the Talmud (English, Hebrew, and Aramaic), Moses ben Jacob Cordovero's *Or Ne'erav*, Steven Lee Beeber's *The Heebie-Jeebies at CBGB's*, Stuart Hall's *The Fateful Triangle*, Lenny Bruce's *How to Talk Dirty and Influence People*, Eli Valley's *Diaspora Boy: Comics on Crisis in America and Israel*, Mezz Mezzrow and Bernard Wolfe's *Really the Blues*, and on and on. Are you excited for the footnotes?

[*Head nods, murmurs of enthusiasm, polite applause.*]

I don't own this stage, but I want you to feel like I do, like you're trapped inside my head. Like you're ... me. I've got my siddur, and my tallit bag, which I take to shul on Saturdays. When I go to temple, when I have the honor of reading from the Torah, I'm called Benyamin Zev. *Benyamin* means to the south, on the south, or on the right hand. *Zev* means wolf. On the right hand—wolf. A sweet gangster name.

Yes, there are Jewish gangsters! Or, at least, there *were* Jewish gangsters when my family landed on the Lower East Side, in the early twentieth century. The streets were ruled by Kid Twist Zwerbach and Cyclone Louie Lewis; the extortion racket was run by the Yiddish Black Hand. Murder Incorporated.

My great-grandparents came to the United States from Eastern Europe, as members of the Hebrew race. That's how they're described in the immigration papers. Why? Hebrew was a racial category. Americans thought of Jews as a race—and as a nation. During the twentieth century, though, Jews in the US became white, like a lot of ethnic groups.

How'd we become white? That's the story I'm telling tonight. And the way I'm telling the story is through music. The evolution of American music is all about the certification of styles, genres, and traditions that *had* been thought of as foreign, primitive, or degraded. Sometimes that happens because musicians insist that the music is—and always has been—American, and sometimes that happens because white faces and voices get attached to the music.

Music teaches us how to be American and how to be white. Music also trains boys to be men. I'm living proof, for better or worse. Music gave me a sense of my masculinity—a claim to my masculinity.

And music showed me the possibilities of expression: how to rebel or conform, how to be myself or become someone else.

To listen to American music is to recognize that who I am—white, male, Gregg—and what that means are always subject to change. Of course, plenty of people would argue that I'm taking the existence of whiteness for granted. They'd argue that being white only means that you're *not* a person of color. Whiteness is like heterosexuality, right? What does "heterosexual" mean? Not gay.

And, actually, that's true! "Heterosexual" exists because of "homosexual," as Eve Sedgwick shows in *Epistemology of the Closet*. Why were these terms created? To define people in opposition to each other, using the arbitrary category of "sexual orientation." Sedgwick makes a very provocative statement, which is at the crux of my politics: everyone's gay, no one's really heterosexual. Go back to Freud's idea of polymorphous perversity, which suggests that the vicissitudes of our sexualities are many and varied. There's the same binary with whiteness—the same use of an arbitrary category to differentiate between people. Except the opposite term is always shifting: what *isn't* white changes as people assimilate, as they learn to identify *others* as belonging to a different race.

White pride, then, is like heterosexual pride: pride in *not* being a person of color, pride in *not* being gay.

We'll return to these themes, I give you my word: all will be revealed! First, though, I want to thank my therapist for coming.

[*Gestures toward the audience with a sweep of his hand; applause.*]

Yes, I'm very grateful. I'm not going to look at or identify my therapist. But I want to say thank you. At $350 per session, the show's not going to go on for more than fifty minutes. Yes, that's right: $350. We take therapy very seriously—it's our version of sports.

Who are *we*? Let's turn to Desmond Dekker's "Israelites," the classic rocksteady song.

> Get up in the morning, slaving for bread, sir
> So that every mouth can be fed
> Poor, poor me Israelites
>
> My wife and my kids, they packed up and leave me
> Darling, she said, I was yours to be seen
> Poor, poor me Israelites
>
> Shirt them a-tear up, trousers are gone
> I don't want to end up like Bonnie and Clyde
> Poor, poor me Israelites
>
> After a storm there must be a calm
> They catch me in the farm

You sound your alarm
Poor, poor me Israelites

I said I get up in the morning, slaving for bread, sir
So that every mouth can be fed
Poor, poor me Israelites

I always wondered: who are the Israelites? The simple answer is in Exodus, which is the first time the Hebrews are referred to as a *people*—and the origin of the idea that Jews belong to a nation. Since then, however, many others have claimed to be the Israelites. Medieval Christians, for instance. The Anglo-Saxons turned Exodus into an epic poem, with Moses and his followers as righteous warriors; they modeled themselves after the Israelites and selected Britain as the promised land, which might have had something to do with justifying an invasion. The original Rastafarians described Africans in the diaspora—the descendants of enslaved people—as Jews, basically: "exiles in Babylon." They imagined a return to the promised land of Ethiopia. Martin Luther King framed the civil rights struggle as a modern-day Exodus, turning the promised land into a metaphor for the state of freedom and equality.

Are we the Israelites? I'm part of an Exodus reading group in New York, and we've been talking about how the story is marshaled to justify acts of conquest or flight. We've also been asking if Exodus describes the conditions of our lives. What does living in Exodus mean? Are we the Israelites, who were enslaved and lost hope, who were enslaved but awakened to the possibility of freedom? Are we wandering through the desert? Have we left what defines us behind, and not yet found what'll define us again?

In the 1980s and '90s, we all wanted to be nomads, thanks to poststructuralism: *I'm not here, I'm not there; I'm in constant movement*. Then nomadism gave way to diaspora. Being part of a diaspora is appealing: it's a way of balancing inheritance and invention; it's a way of understanding oneself in relation to others that doesn't hinge on the right to a piece of land. Being part of a diaspora works for me.

I come from Queens, and I don't have any other place to go back to, really. I don't plan on returning to Queens; I have no claim to territory in my homeland. I don't feel like I'm in Exodus, like I'm kept away from the piece of earth that'll make me whole. I do spend my days wandering, though, and wherever I appear I present a different aspect of myself, which is a pleasure and a privilege. I can be shameless or inhibited, manic or depressive. Every step is a throw of the dice.

Stuart Hall, one of my intellectual heroes, argues that all identities are based on race, ethnicity, and nation—the "fateful triangle." You have to understand each in terms of the other; you can't disentangle them. This is extremely, urgently important, given that so many people in the United States are fixated on blood and soil, right? Race, ethnicity, and nation are made up—they're cultural and historical inventions, without much of a basis in material reality—and yet they determine who people are and how they treat each other. Race, ethnicity, and nation are constructions, but they shape the world.

Hall talks about diaspora in the same way: as a matter of imagination as well as circumstance. To Hall, being in the diaspora means embracing the fact that you don't belong in one place or another. Going from Africa to the Caribbean and then migrating to London or New York means you're not defined by what's inherited from your parents or imposed by your nation. Being in the diaspora means having a sense of "dislocation," which is also a source of freedom. If you've got no homeland to return to, you have to figure out another path.

In 1970, the Jewish philosopher and rabbi Emil Fackenheim published *God's Presence in History*, which responds to the Holocaust by arguing that Jews are "commanded to survive as Jews." He describes Jewish identity as threefold: religious, cultural, and national. I've always dwelled on the religious and the cultural aspects of Jewishness.

The national character of Jewish identity is interesting to me, but ... I'm not going to pretend there isn't a state—a so-called Jewish state—that's oppressing people who live on the same land but aren't Jews. I'm not going to pretend that Fackenheim's insistence on the security of Israel, as a safeguard against another genocide, hasn't been co-opted by an ethnonationalist movement.

The Torah doesn't refer to Israel as a country, much less the country that currently exists in Palestine. The Torah refers to a people in diaspora, a people on the march. Of course, it's hard to live in the diaspora; the diaspora is where you end up if you're displaced. And that means you're vulnerable: you're subject to the whims of whichever state is willing to accept you, to the opening and closing of borders.

That said, I happen to like the diaspora. I'm content in the diaspora. To me, there's something beautiful, even heroic, about holding on to your culture and beliefs while allowing them to be malleable, open to the influence of wherever you find yourself. And there's something powerful about being mobile: you can travel with your culture; you can adapt to a different country, city, and neighborhood; you can think and speak in another language.

You can also get beat up by kids who don't look like you—or don't like the way you look. I grew up in a neighborhood that was Jewish, Black, Puerto Rican, Italian, and Korean. What bound us together? We were all working class and we were all trying to get out. We were all American and we were all something other than American.

Personally, I did *not* understand myself as American. What was I? Honestly, I was confused. My family was American inasmuch as we had no other national identity, no allegiance to Israel. Of course, my grandparents would be horrified by what I'm saying: they fought to be Americans. They struggled to get to the United States from Russia, Poland, and Romania, and then the men went to war in Europe and Asia while the women worked at home. The horror of the war—the horror of the Holocaust—brought about a crisis of conscience, which took on force with the rise of the civil rights movement. Would Jews resist or accept the bargain on offer, the promise of belonging? What would they have to sacrifice in exchange?

I grew up with the question of the status of the Jews—of our family—hovering. Only the grandparents and great-grandparents talked about the old country, but I was acutely aware of my family coming from somewhere else. We spoke Yiddish and English: Yiddish when we were at home, English when we went out. We lived in New York City, but Manhattan was as far away—and as glamorous—as Hollywood. We were in Brooklyn, then Queens; we took the express train to get to America. My grandparents lived in Kew Gardens, Queens, for thirty years, and my grandmother went to Manhattan twice.

My grandfather worked at a clock factory in Flatiron, but he didn't know anything about Manhattan beyond the neighborhood. He was a sweet, gentle, and hardworking man. He woke up at five o'clock every morning to take the bus to the train to the factory, which was on Twenty-Fifth Street and Broadway. He wasn't a clockmaker, he wasn't an intellectual; he read the *Daily News*. I remember riding the subway with him and saying, "Why do you read the *Daily News*? You'll learn a lot more if you read the *New York Times*." He said, "I don't need to know that much."

I learned a lot from that, actually—I learned a lot about his world.

My grandfather wanted me to become a rabbi. The options, in descending order, were doctor, lawyer, and rabbi. I was afraid of blood, so doctor was out. Did I seem like a promising lawyer? My family wasn't exactly testing my IQ or debating my aptitudes. I had no depth as a child. I might as well have been a cardboard cutout who occasionally got larger and required new clothing. But I got academic honors and I excelled in Hebrew school. I was talented, as the rabbi told my parents, and desperate to fit in, desperate to be accepted.

By the time I was twelve, rabbi was the top contender. My grandfather was pleased. He was like, "They give you a house!" Then, at my school, which was public but very Jewish—closed for high holidays—I came across a book of stories about inspiring Jews. One of them was about young Robert Zimmerman, who grew up to be Bob Dylan. *I, too, could be a rock star!*

I decided to forget about being a doctor, lawyer, or rabbi; I'd be a rock star. Unfortunately, as you can see, I failed. I became an artist. I chose to do whatever I'm doing now: sitting here, sweating bullets, talking to you.

I started working on this show two weeks after Heather Heyer was killed in Charlottesville in the summer of 2017, as white supremacists and neo-Nazis marched with torches, chanting, "Jews will not replace us." This confounded me. Why do they think we're going to replace them? How? Do I want their jobs, their lives? I had to google "Jews will not replace us." I found an article in the *Washington Post* that explained the phrase very clearly: the fascists who are chanting believe that Black and brown people are coming to the US in such great numbers, and reproducing at such a rapid clip, that white Americans will soon be outnumbered. They believe the campaign is being organized by the Jews: "non-white imposters."

Faced with neo-Nazis up in arms over the great replacement, white genocide, white extinction, and so on, I decided to go out and do the most Jewish show possible. I decided to take my queer Jewish act on the road, *schmear* myself in *schmaltz*, and grease up the fucking world.

[*Hoots and hollers of approval from the audience.*]

Schmaltz is chicken fat, which, where I come from, you *schmear* on bread. Very tasty!

I grew up with schmaltz—and I grew up with the Holocaust. I can hardly remember a time when I didn't know about the Nazis and the concentration camps. We watched Alain Resnais's *Night and Fog* in Hebrew school when I was nine years old! We had family friends, Yetta and Max Rosenberg, with numbers from a concentration camp tattooed on their arms. Max was the *shammash* at our Orthodox temple: the helper, the one who sings louder and earlier than everybody else, to keep them in time. Yetta was a tailor and seamstress who worked from home. One summer day, when I was eight or nine, we went over to pick up some clothes. Max always wore long-sleeve shirts, even in the summer, but

Yetta was wearing a dress with short sleeves. I'd never seen her tattoo before, and I asked my mother what the number meant. She had to explain the Holocaust to me.

From then on, I had a notion that I was ethically—or ethnically—bound to bear witness to the experiences of the people in my community who, like Yetta and Max, had endured such great suffering. Yetta and Max had the numbers on their arms and I, too, had to give witness and testimony.

Here I am: Benyamin Zev, offering testimony. Good Shabbos! How many of you are *shomer* Shabbos? No one. Because it's Friday night and you're here, right? None of us are *frum*, none of us are observant. But we'll stay in the zone of observance, since this is a holy night.

Shabbos is when we welcome the *Shechinah*, the feminine aspect of G-d. Did you know that G-d has two aspects, at least? At least! Get out of the binary. You won't find that in the Talmud, though; if you want to get out of the binary, you've got to read Kabbalah, which describes the Shechinah as the Sabbath bride. We welcome her; we honor her; we rejoice at her presence.

The feminine aspect of divinity isn't often recognized by Jews—or by people who think about Jews—but it's part of the religion. Judaism is patriarchal, unfortunately, but the understanding of gender isn't so conventional or straightforward. Historically, the ideal for Orthodox Jews is that men study all the time and women work. Men handle the spiritual aspects of life; women handle the material aspects of life. Men stay at home and go to yeshiva; women deal with money, which means they travel for business, meet people beyond the community, and see the world. Men wear finery—satin, silk, fur—and women conceal themselves with frumpy dresses and wigs.

Beyond the Hasidic enclaves around the world, these gender roles are vestigial in Jewish culture. And, unsurprisingly, so are the anti-Semitic tropes that characterize Jewish men as weak and womanly. If only I'd known, as an overweight, bookish, effete child, that I was being taunted because of confusion in the Old World about circumcision versus castration!

Unfortunately, I took many years to develop into the extremely cool person who now sits before you, and in that time I often dealt with the age-old question: what's going on with Jewish men and their penises? I admit to entertaining the same question! As a Jewish boy, I had a certain amount of latitude around effeminacy. You won't be surprised to learn that I did a drag act at home from five to nine years old. I'd go into my grandmother's closet, get a headscarf, shawl, and clip-on earrings, and play an elderly woman from the old country.

[*Mimes pulling a scarf over his head, contorts his face so as to resemble an elderly woman.*]

My family loved it. I killed with that act! But around the time I turned nine, my parents pulled me aside and said, "Enough, Gregg. Really. We got it. Enough with the..." They didn't say *drag*, but I was heavily discouraged. I tried to do the act a few more times, but the family was unified. They wouldn't clap anymore, even though they'd found it hilarious for years. A great career was ruined.

When I was fifteen or sixteen, I violated the ban—I started using mascara. Instead of trying to look like a *bubbe*, I was trying to look like Lou Reed. I'd bought *Transformer* at Mays department store on Union Square and everything had changed: I wrote "Lou Reed is G-d" on the cover of the denim looseleaf binder that I carried around at school. I spent hours sitting on my bed, listening to *Transformer*.

[*Sings quietly into the microphone.*]

"Candy came from out on the Island / In the back room, she was everybody's darling."

I stared at the front cover with Lou Reed in mascara. Then I flipped the LP and stared at the pictures on the back cover. On the right was an East Village clone in a tight white T-shirt, painted-on Levi's with a huge bulge in the crotch, a leather hat, and engineer boots. On the left was a femme fatale in a red dress with gorgeous, flowing brunette hair.

I imagined a world based on those pictures—and a role for me in that world—as I listened to *Transformer* over and over and over again.

> Holly came from Miami, FLA
> Hitchhiked her way across the USA
> Plucked her eyebrows on the way
> Shaved her legs and then he was a she
>
> She says, "Hey babe, take a walk on the wild side"
> Said, "Hey honey, take a walk on the wild side"
>
> Candy came from out on the Island
> In the backroom, she was everybody's darling
> But she never lost her head
> Even when she was giving head
>
> She says, "Hey babe, take a walk on the wild side"
> Said, "Hey babe, take a walk on the wild side"
>
> And the colored girls go: Doo-doo-doo, doo-doo
> Doo-doo-doo, doo, doo-doo, doo-doo
>
> ...
>
> Little Joe never once gave it away
> Everybody had to pay and pay
> A hustle here and a hustle there
> New York City is the place where they said

> "Hey babe, take a walk on the wild side"
> I said, "Hey Joe, take a walk on the wild side"

If you look back and forth at the covers of the LP, like I did, you come to think that the pictures are all of the same person. I was fascinated: I studied the resemblances and the differences. For hours and hours, I listened to *Transformer* and tried to wrap my mind around the possibility that the pictures were of the same person—or that the three figures were aspects of the same person. I started to form an idea of masculinity that merged Jewishness with queerness. I realized that my identity was based on how I appeared to others, how I imagined myself as appearing to others, and how I appeared to myself.

Why was Lou Reed so important to me? Reed was a prophet: he'd trekked into the desert, his head full of anger, confusion, and questions, and he'd returned with the revelation. He'd come back and spoken to those of us who most needed the message. When I first heard Reed on the radio, I genuinely thought he was singing to me. And I still thought he was singing to me seventeen years later, when I went with fellow AIDS activists to see him at the Beacon. We needed to hear the voice of the wilderness; we needed to feel the sense of purpose that comes from being in contact with divinity. So we headed to the Upper West Side to receive the prophesy of the *New York* album. Here's what Reed told us:

This is no time for celebration
This is no time for shaking hands
This is no time for backslapping
This is no time for marching bands

This is no time for optimism
This is no time for endless thought
This is no time for my country right or wrong
Remember what that brought

There is no time
There is no time
There is no time
There is no time

This is no time for congratulations
This is no time to turn your back
This is no time for circumlocution
This is no time for learned speech

This is no time to count your blessings
This is no time for private gain
This is the time to put up or shut up
It won't come back this way again

Why else was Lou Reed important to me? Well, he's from Long Island, I'm from Long Island. He's queer, I'm queer. He was seen on the Chelsea piers in the 1970s. He had three heterosexual marriages and a years-long relationship with a trans woman named Rachel. He was very public about the relationship, which is amazing, really, given the era. Rachel managed the production of the *Berlin* album and the tour that followed. Reed went to clubs with Rachel, talked about her, and hosted parties with her. They even had a fake wedding with a three-tier cake in 1977. Reed sang about her, too. At the end of "Coney Island Baby," Reed says: "I'd like to send this one out to Lou and Rachel / ... Man, I swear, I'd give the whole thing up for you."

I moved to Manhattan because of Lou Reed. I got an apartment in the East Village in 1982. And, taking after Lou, I began my peripatetic sex life. I started out as an anarchist sex radical: *Don't put labels on me! I'm gonna love who I want to love!*

I was promiscuous in many ways—musically, especially. I had no aesthetic fidelity to anything. I'd go to the A7 club and see the Young and the Useless, which became the Beastie Boys, then I'd go the Pyramid Club to see Lady Bunny and Taboo!, who were drag queens, and I'd take drugs and dance to gay disco. I'd go to Danceteria and see James Chance and the Contortions. (I remember someone putting a beer on the stage and Chance kicking the bottle like a football into the audience, hitting some poor schlub on the head. *His* stage! Don't mess around.) I'd go to the Roxy—now I'm just bragging—and see Afrika Bambaataa and Zulu Nation on the wheels of steel, Grandmaster Flash with Melle Mel.

Why choose? I didn't choose between rock and roll and disco, hip-hop and punk. I don't choose between

Chicago pizza and New York pizza. Why choose? That's my response to most dilemmas in life. *Why choose?* Just flip the LP over and over and over again.

Somebody asked me the other day, "What were you during the '80s?" Was I punk? Honestly, I was a poser, OK? I was a poser, I was a fraud. I wasn't a punk. But punk music saved me. Punk music, for me, was a style of masculinity that embraced irony around ethnic identity and ambiguity around sexuality. People who couldn't play instruments could be rock stars, and people who didn't look like rock stars could be rock stars. Joey Ramone!

I know someone who kissed Joey Ramone. She's in the room—I'm not going to say who, because it's not my story. *I* didn't kiss Joey Ramone. He had fish lips.

The Ramones, of course, were from Queens. Joey Ramone and Tommy Ramone, the drummer, were Jews. Joey was born as Jeffrey Hyman, and Tommy, an Orthodox immigrant from Hungary, was born as Tamás Erdély. The Ramones' manager, Danny Fields, was born as Daniel Feinberg. Why did all these Jewish kids from the boroughs move to downtown Manhattan and form punk bands? Because they didn't want to be defined by ethnicity—or, at least, by ethnicity as defined by others. They didn't want to choose between assimilation and isolation. And they realized that, as a punk band, they could amplify some stereotypes and demolish others; they could dress like street gangs from Queens and infantry from Munich. They could be whomever they wanted. They could be misunderstood.

Who knows the Dictators? A famous Queens punk outfit—all Jews. Which is hilarious, at least to a very small group of people. The real name of the singer, Handsome Dick Manitoba? Richard Blum. He and his bar mitzvahed bandmates went so far as to fashion themselves as the Nazi dolts of 1970s America in "Master Race Rock."

> Hippies are squares with long hair
> And they don't wear no underwear
> Country rock is on the wane
> I don't want music, I want pain!
>
> Dictators can swing
> Make you dance and sing
> Cause an oil spill
> You don't know us, but you will!
>
> We're the members of the master race
> Got no style, and we got no grace
> Sleep all night, sleep all day
> Nothing good on TV anyway
>
> ...
>
> We're the members of the master race
> We don't judge you by your face
> First we check to see what you eat
> Then we bend down and smell your feet

I saw the Dictators play, of course. At CBGB? Gildersleeves? Some dive.

Like a lot of Jewish punks in New York, the Dictators were known for sporting swastikas. Before the Ramones took the stage at CBGB in 1974, dressed in black leather jackets, looking like the SS, everyone in New York was wearing brown and suede. Then came the swastikas. Why? In England, the punks wore swastikas as a fuck-you to their parents, the World War II generation. They were rejecting the world their parents had made, the values they'd professed, the fascists they'd enabled. Malcolm McLaren, the Jewish manager of the Sex Pistols, and his girlfriend, Vivienne Westwood, were notorious for making shirts and armbands printed with swastikas, modeled by Johnny Rotten and Sid Vicious—and sold at the couple's bondage boutique, of course.

Susan Sontag wrote very persuasively about the Nazi uniforms in "Fascinating Fascism":

> SS uniforms were stylish, well-cut, with a touch (but not too much) of eccentricity. Compare the rather boring and not very well cut American army uniform: jacket, shirt, tie, pants, socks, and lace-up shoes—essentially civilian clothes no matter how bedecked with medals and badges. SS uniforms were tight, heavy, stiff and included gloves to confine the hands and boots that made legs and feet feel heavy, encased, obliging their wearer to stand up straight.

If you were a Jewish kid who grew up in New York, getting your slacks hemmed by a woman with a concentration-camp tattoo, what was the worst thing you could do to piss off your parents? Wear a swastika. Play a song called "Master Race Rock" or "Blitzkrieg Bop." That was the protest: not only pissing off your family, but taking control of the symbols of anti-Semitism, mocking the Nazis, and confusing everyone. The reversal of the swastika in the time of the floating signifier.

Personally, I couldn't do it. I couldn't wear a swastika. I understood the irony, but I couldn't help but think of Max and Yetta.

The Stooges wore swastikas on stage, and at one concert Iggy Pop dedicated "Rich Bitch" to all the "Hebrew women" in the crowd. A lot of people think Iggy—James Newell Osterberg Jr.—is Jewish. Nah. His father was adopted by Jews who were fleeing the Holocaust, and that's why his name is Osterberg. Who else? Richard Meyers, aka Richard Hell—he was raised with no religion and he doesn't really identify as Jewish, which is his choice, but his father was Jewish. And he was part of the Jewish downtown punk milieu. So was Lenny Kaye—Lenny Kusikov—of the Patti Smith Group. Before he started playing with Smith, Kaye was hired by Elektra Records to put together a two-volume anthology of garage rock called *Nuggets: Original Artyfacts from the First Psychedelic Era, 1965–1968.* "I like to think of myself as a scholar of the Talmud of rock and roll," he said.

Nuggets became the playbook of New York punk: everyone covered songs from the collection. The Beau Brummels, Paul Revere & the Raiders, the Chocolate Watchband, the Electric Prunes, and Strawberry Alarm Clock—those bands were the ancient rabbis, and the punks acted as commentators. I'm especially partial to the Cramps's interpretation of "Psychotic Reaction," a tractate by Count Five—an enormously influential song for me.

> I feel depressed, I feel so bad
> 'Cause you're the best girl that I ever had

If you think I'm going to dance, I'm not. All right—maybe a little.

[*Dances tentatively.*]

> I can't get your love, I can't get satisfaction
> Uh-oh, little girl, psychotic reaction
> And it feels like this!

I don't know what that's called. Here's the Watusi.

[*Shimmies.*]

> I feel so lonely night and day
> I can't get your love, I must stay away
> I need you girl, by my side

Now the Pony.

[*Vigorously wriggles, then coughs, gasps.*]

Uh-oh ... I'm old. I'm fifty-four. And I smoke. I apologize for being old and out of breath. Besides not choosing when presented with a dilemma—my mantra is "Yes, and..."—what's gotten me through life are: coffee, cigarettes, and denial. Denial is a perfectly natural psychological mechanism, and I highly recommend it.

> Uh-oh, little girl with the lovin' inside
> I can't get your love, I can't get an itty-bitty fraction
> Uh-oh, little girl, psychotic reaction

All hail the Talmud of rock and roll! All hail Lenny Kaye! All hail the Cramps!

Who loves the Cramps? I saw the Cramps, of course: Peppermint Lounge, 1984. I arrived five hours early—maybe four hours, maybe three—so I could be in the front row. At some point, I reached up and I grabbed Lux Interior's boot. I swear to G-d. He then blessed my forehead with his heel, sending me back to where I belonged. I was sore, but I was honored to have communed with Erick Lee Purkhiser—another Jew dismaying his parents, obviously.

Why am I outing all these Jews? (If you were wearing MAGA hats, this would go over just as well!) Lou Reed, the Ramones, the Dictators, Lenny

Kaye—these are aspirational stories for the era before multiculturalism, when Jews had to assimilate in order to join the mainstream. Leather jackets and swastikas or suits and briefcases. Robert Zimmerman, Joey Ramone, and Malcolm McLaren or Bernie Madoff, Harvey Weinstein, and Roy Cohn.

Fellow Jews would never out Cohn as gay, but they'd out him as Jewish; they'd hold him up as a model. *You, too, could be Jewish, gay, and a high-priced lawyer for fascists!*

No one ever said to me, as a child: "Gregg, you could be the next Roy Cohn!" Cohn was evil; he was a race traitor, he'd tortured Jews—suspected communists—before Congress. Telling your kids to be like Cohn would be like saying: "Honey, sweetheart, if you work hard and play by the rules, you could grow up to be a movie mogul like Harvey Weinstein, or a financier like Bernie Madoff!" Nevertheless, I grew up with the sense that, as a Jew, you had a decision to make: you could go along with the consolidation of whiteness or you could take your place among the minorities on the margins. You could shed your name, history, and language or you could eat TV dinners in Queens. You could wear a suit or mend other people's suits.

My parents and grandparents put an enormous amount of pressure on me to professionalize. I was the oldest son, the oldest grandson. I was smart: I won awards, I got academic honors. And, at that point, there weren't many pathways available to Jews in the United States. There weren't many role models who hadn't chosen assimilation over misery. I remember trying to come up with names: Bob Dylan and ... Albert Einstein? Unfortunately, according to my parents, I wasn't going to be the next Dylan. And I *definitely* wasn't going to be the next Einstein.

Like many American Jews, my family was ambivalent about assimilation—about the constant drive to recruit new groups to the cause of whiteness. My family was working class and progressive; they supported the civil rights struggle and opposed the Vietnam War. But they never talked about themselves as nonwhite, even though they were defined by an ethnic identity that they understood as ... nonwhite. They experienced the transition of Jews from Hebrew foreigners into white Americans, but they maintained a reasonably paranoid sense of the world being against them. They didn't have access to the idea of disidentification, to use José Esteban Muñoz's term; they didn't have a sense of what to do or not do with their newfound whiteness.

The question of what to do with your whiteness—whether to identify or disidentify—resonates for me, given the political moment. I get the sense that the fascists and neo-Nazis in this country aren't too interested in joining forces—or bloodlines—with Jews. But they are working to reinforce white supremacy as white people become the minority, because they need to widen the aperture of whiteness in order to maintain control, in order to uphold racial capitalism. The neo-Nazis who marched in Charlottesville—and those who watched and made excuses, or said nothing—are animated by the fantasy of whiteness, which they'll pursue by carrying on the grand tradition of parsing ethnicities. They'll use lineage, genetics, skin color, character, etc. to determine who is and isn't white, and to turn people against each other.

I'm assuming you're against that? I'm making an assumption about my audience.

In my twenties, after I'd moved to New York, I came across a book called *Really the Blues*, the autobiography of Mezz Mezzrow, as told to the sociologist Bernard Wolf. Who's heard of Mezzrow? He was born as Milton, a Jewish Chicagoan, in the 1890s; he got in trouble as a teenager for stealing a car and learned saxophone at reform school. He moved to New Orleans, then New York, balancing crime and jazz, bootlegging and producing records. Eventually, he became Louis Armstrong's arranger.

Wolf was fascinated by Mezzrow because he not only disavowed his whiteness, he decided he was Black. He devoted himself to Black music, married a Black woman, and occasionally passed as Black. He identified as a Black man, calling himself a "voluntary Negro."

Here's a cut he made with Sidney Bechet, "The Blues and Freud."

[*Musical break.*]

Mezzrow's achievements went beyond music: he was the preeminent pot dealer in Harlem, where "Mezz" was a synonym for a joint. There's a recording of Armstrong—one of Mezzrow's best customers—counting out a song and saying, "Mezz, Mezz, Mezzarola."

Does anyone say "Mezz" anymore? What do the kids call a joint these days?

[*Looks at the audience, waits for an answer.*]

Oh, right. You vape.

When I first read *Really the Blues*, I made the connection between Mezzrow—the "voluntary Negro"—and Yiddish swing, which was a phenomenon on the radio in the 1920s and '30s. Yiddish swing emerges from klezmer music, which is often called Jewish jazz. But, in the beginning, klezmer didn't actually have anything to do with jazz. Klezmer was Eastern European folk music. When Jewish musicians moved to New York, though, they went to the clubs, hung out with the musicians, and picked up the sounds and styles of jazz. Eventually, they created Yiddish swing by adapting the idiom of jazz to Yiddish songs.

Yiddish swing was the soundtrack of my grandparents' home: I'd go over and dance to records by the Barry Sisters. (Yes, my grandmother taught me to dance.) Have you heard of the Barry Sisters? Also known as the Bagelman Sisters?

Come on! They were the Dixie Chicks of the Jewish diaspora! Two Ashkenazi girls from the Bronx whose parents emigrated from Kiev. The sisters started to perform on the radio in the 1930s, but they didn't record until much later. They played the Catskills resort circuit, they appeared on *The Ed Sullivan Show* and *The Tonight Show*—they even toured the Soviet Union. Singing in Yiddish, they covered all kinds of famous songs, from ballads to show tunes, from "Raindrops Keep Falling on My Head" to "Cabaret." And they started with Yiddish swing.

When I moved to Manhattan and started seeing all the Jewish punk musicians at downtown clubs, I got interested in the history of Jews in rock and roll, which stems from rhythm and blues, which is an

African American art form. I read about Jews entering into American culture by way of Black music. And I asked: what was I listening to when I was listening to the Barry Sisters?

Rock and roll is theft, right? White people stealing from the music of African Americans: rhythm and blues, soul, gospel, and jazz. Jazz came out of African American culture, which was largely segregated from what white people heard, saw, and read. For Black music to be integrated into white American culture, there had to be a white face on the album cover. You know the story. But Yiddish swing is more complicated. When the genre came into being, American Jews weren't quite American, and they weren't likely to identify as white. They were listening to Yiddish radio stations, but they were also cosmopolitan; many of them had come of age during the cultural ferment in Weimar Germany. They were primed to embrace and incorporate all kinds of vernacular.

When I hear Yiddish swing, I think: only in the diaspora! And only on the radio. American Jews were linked to each other, and to shared traditions, by the radio, which also exposed them to jazz, along with so many other aspects of American culture.

The ultimate example is the song "Bay Mir Bistu Sheyn," which means, literally, "By Me, You Look

Beautiful." Great, right? Here's the 1973 recording of the Barry Sisters doing the song in Yiddish, which was always on rotation at my grandparents' house:

[*Lyrics are translated from the Yiddish.*]

> Of all the boys I've known, and I've known some
> Until I first met you, I was lonesome
> And when you came in sight, dear, my heart grew light
> And this old world seemed new to me
>
> You're really swell, I have to admit, you
> Deserve expressions that really fit you
> And so I've racked my brain, hoping to explain
> All the things that you do to me
>
> Bay mir bistu sheyn, please let me explain
> Bay mir bistu sheyn means you're grand
> Bay mir bistu sheyn, again I'll explain
> It means you're the fairest in the land
>
> I could say, "Bella, bella," even say, "Wunderbar"
> Each language only helps me tell you how grand you are
>
> I've tried to explain "bay mir bistu sheyn"
> So kiss me and say you understand

"Bay Mir Bistu Sheyn" has been recorded in English by dozens of famous singers, but most people don't know that the song was originally written for a Yiddish musical at a Brooklyn theater in 1932. The song was a hit on the Yiddish circuit for a season, then disappeared until the Andrews Sisters recorded the English version—more of a bastardization than a translation—in 1937. The Barry Sisters went with the lyrics from the Andrews Sisters version, which pales in comparison to the original. Here's a taste of the original, written for a Yiddish-speaking audience with a penchant for cruelty:

> Even if you had a Tatar complexion
> Even if you had tomcat eyes
> And even if you had a little limp
> Or had wooden legs
> I would say, "It doesn't bother me."

Somehow, the Andrews Sisters record topped the charts, then became a global sensation: every Yiddish act covered the song, and the English version was performed by Ella Fitzgerald, Judy Garland, and Benny Goodman. "Bay Mir Bistu Sheyn" exploded on German radio after the Nazis banned music by Jewish composers—apparently, the DJs didn't know Yiddish from a southern German dialect. After the Nazis took "Bay Mir Bistu Sheyn" off the air, the Soviet Union used the tune for an anti-German propaganda song. The translations went in every direction.

I listened to the Barry Sisters with my grandparents, but I grew up in a Motown household. I came home and switched from Yiddish musicals to my mom's stack of 45s: Martha and the Vandellas, the Supremes, Ronnie and the Ronettes. We had a great stereo because my stepfather worked for KLH, the speaker company top of-the-line speakers.

We'd meet in the living room of our two-bedroom apartment in Queens, put on a 45, and dance—or, at least, me and my mom would. She taught me to dance the Watusi, the Pony, and the Lindy Hop. We danced to Sly and the Family Stone, the Four Tops, and the Temptations. How could we not dance to "Papa Was a Rolling Stone"?

> It was the third of September
> That day I'll always remember, yes I will
> 'Cause that was the day that my daddy died
> I never got a chance to see him
> Never heard nothing but bad things about him
> Mama, I'm depending on you to tell me the truth
> Mama just hung her head and said
>
> "Son, Papa was a rolling stone
> Wherever he laid his hat was his home
> (And when he died)
> All he left us was a loan
> Papa was a rolling stone, my son
> Wherever he laid his hat was his home
> (And when he died)
> All he left us was a loan"
> Well, well
>
> Hey Mama, is it true what they say
> That Papa never worked a day in his life?
> And Mama, some bad talk going around town
> Saying that Papa had three outside children
> And another wife and that ain't right
> I heard some talk about Papa doing some
> storefront preaching

> Talking about saving souls and all the time leeching
> Dealing in debt and stealing in the name of the Lord
> Mama just hung her head and said

My father was a musician, remember? He left us for somewhere better. He left us for ... music. My stepdad worked at the speaker factory. He was *never* going to leave us. He adopted me! He didn't speak to his parents for ten years because they disapproved of him marrying a divorced woman with a child. And he got us a great record collection, mostly by taking promos home from the factory.

Basically, my stepdad was doomed. I had this huge structuring absence: my glamorous father who'd gone off to live his dream and make music. I used to sit on the stoop in Queens, watch the men who passed, and imagine my father coming home.

Harstein was a legend. My mom's favorite memories were of my dad. When my stepfather wasn't around, my mom would tell me the story of how she went with my dad to Trude Heller's in the Village and got to play Max Roach's drums after a late-night set. She went with him to see Dizzy Gillespie at Madison Square Garden. My stepfather—I could never get with his style. He was a really nice guy, but he liked hippie music; he liked Canned Heat.

I will *not* play Canned Heat for you—it's like the soundtrack for a Geico commercial.

[*Sings Canned Heat's "On the Road Again."*]

Ugh. Even as a child, I absolutely hated that music.

[*Looks for his analyst in the audience.*]

I know, I know—we'll take this up in therapy.

I admit that I wanted to follow my father. I wanted to go where he'd gone: to music. Thankfully, Lou Reed showed me another path, another way of being myself. He changed my life. Really, though, the radio changed my life; the album *Transformer*—a commodity manufactured by RCA Records—changed my life. I changed when I heard the advertisement for *Transformer* on the radio in 1972.

> [*Reed sings.*]
>
> We're coming out
> Out of our closets
> Out on the streets
>
> [*Narrator speaks.*]
>
> In the midst of all the make-believe madness, the mock depravity, and the pseudosexual anarchists, Lou Reed is the real thing.
>
> [*Reed sings.*]
>
> Vicious
> You want me to hit you with a stick
> But all I've got's a guitar pick

[*Narrator speaks.*]

Lou Reed—the original. He's been one since the birth of the New York underground. And now he's back with a new album, *Transformer.*

[*Reed sings.*]

I said, "Hey honey, take a walk on the wild side"
And the colored girls say ...

[*Narrator speaks.*]

Transformer, a new album by the original: Lou Reed. Produced by David Bowie. On RCA Records and Tapes

The transmission of culture—from downtown clubs and lofts to my bedroom in Queens, where I played the record over and over again—via airwaves and record shops, beyond the control of the authorities, however tainted by commercialism, made me move to Manhattan when I was eighteen. *Transformer* and Emile de Antonio's *Painters Painting*, which I saw in high school. (I was very precocious.) How many people have seen *Painters Painting*? You should! There are some Jews in the movie: Barnett Newman, Helen Frankenthaler, Hilton Kramer, Clement Greenberg. Don't trust me, though. Once, at a party, I was very drunk and I convinced everyone that Bruce Springsteen was Jewish.

Reed—along with Newman and Greenberg—exposed me to a world beyond my shtetl. And that says something about the power of the radio. Reed testifies in the Velvet Underground song "Rock and Roll":

> Jenny said when she was just five years old
> There was nothing happening at all
> Every time she puts on a radio
> There was a nothin' goin' down at all
> Not at all
> Then one fine mornin' she puts on a New York station
> You know, she couldn't believe what she heard at all
> She started shakin' to that fine, fine music
> You know her life was saved by rock 'n' roll
>
> Despite all the amputations
> You know you could just go out
> And dance to a rock 'n' roll station
>
> ...
>
> Jenny said when she was just about five years old
> You know my parents gonna be the death of us all
> Two TV sets and two Cadillac cars
> Well you know, it ain't gonna help me at all
> Not just a tiny bit
> Then one fine mornin' she turns on a New York station
> She doesn't believe what she hears at all
> Ooh, she started dancin' to that fine, fine music
> You know her life is saved by
> Rock 'n' roll
> Yeah, rock 'n' roll
>
> Despite all the computations
> You could just dance
> To that rock 'n' roll station

I know, I know, it's not the same anymore. You have Spotify.

[*Bows head and sings.*]

"She started dancin' to that fine, fine playlist / You know her life was saved by Discover Weekly."

Don't worry, I'm not going to go on and on about the death of radio. But in order to explain how I became who I am, I have to tell you about my experience of the death of radio, and how the radio gave birth to new technologies, new forms of transmission. I have to talk about being a fat, lonely, brainy queer kid who listens to music in his room and gets beat on.

Can I get a witness?

I have to talk about my girlfriend teaching me to shop for jewelry at the pet store, cut my hair without looking in the mirror, and wear ripped-up jeans and T-shirts.

Can I get a witness?

I have to talk about the radio as salvation. How else would I have known to buy *Transformer*? How else would I have known to stay away from the pseudo-sexual anarchists (until, at forty, I became one)?!?

To me, the radio represented freedom. And mobility—a very modern idea, which I understood as having as much to do with diaspora as rock and roll. I was always caught between tradition and radical self-invention, between feeling rooted and feeling displaced, between getting away from something and moving toward something. So, of course, I have to play Jonathan Richman, the front man of the Modern Lovers, praising the radio in "Roadrunner":

> Roadrunner, roadrunner
> Going faster miles an hour
> Gonna drive past the Stop 'n' Shop
> With the radio on
> I'm in love with Massachusetts
> And the neon when it's cold outside
> And the highway when it's late at night
> Got the radio on
> I'm like the roadrunner
>
> Alright
> I'm in love with modern moonlight
> 128 when it's dark outside
> I'm in love with Massachusetts
> I'm in love with the radio on
> It helps me from being alone late at night
> It helps me from being lonely late at night
> I don't feel so bad now in the car
> Don't feel so alone, got the radio on
> Like the roadrunner
> That's right
>
> Said welcome to the spirit of 1956
> Patient in the bushes next to '57
> The highway is your girlfriend as you go by quick
> Suburban trees, suburban speed
> And it smells like heaven (thunder)

And I say roadrunner once
Roadrunner twice
I'm in love with rock & roll and I'll be out all night
Roadrunner
That's right

Two styles of masculinity. Richman is a vegetarian who wore a crew cut and chinos and didn't like drugs; a nice Jewish boy. And Reed is a druggie who was mean to everyone; a nasty asshole. In "I'm Straight," Richman sings to a girl with a boyfriend named "hippie Johnny," who's "always stoned." Richman's ethos is punk, and he's like: why can't Johnny face reality? But Richman loved Reed, and even traveled to New York to be around him, sleeping on the Velvet Underground's manager's couch and hanging out at Warhol's Factory.

Richman owed his life to Reed. Why? Because he listened to the radio. Richman gets Talmudic on Reed in "Velvet Underground," his reading of the band and the genre of rock and roll. Richman is the son of immigrants, a proud American, and he turns the Velvet Underground into an unlikely avatar of the country.

They were wild like the USA
A mystery band in a New York way
Rock and roll, but not like the rest
And, to me, America at its best
How in the world were they making that sound?
Velvet Underground

...

Twangy sounds of the cheapest types,
Sounds as stark as black and white stripes,
Bold and brash, sharp and rude,
Like the heats turned off
And you're low on food
How in the world were they making that sound?
Velvet Underground
Like this:

Doc and Sally inside
She's cooking for the down five
She's staring at Miss Rayon
She's busy licking up her pusher's hand
I'm searching for my mainline
I said I couldn't hit it sideways
I said I couldn't hit it sideways
She does it just like Sister Ray said
All right

Wild wild parties when they start to unwind
A close encounter of the thirdest kind
On the bandstand playing, everybody's saying
How in the world were they making that sound?
Velvet Underground.

You'll notice that, when Richman switches over to the Talmudic quotation of the Velvet Underground—"Like this"—he plays the chords and sings the lyrics from "Sister Ray." He's improvising; he's imitating Reed but he ends up skewering him, too. The effect is comical: a nice, straitlaced, vegetarian Jewish boy reimagining Reed's meditation on heroin and transcendence. In the process, though, Richman gets at some classic American themes, right? He turns an edgy song about drugs and the gritty streets of New York City into an anthem for the suburban kids who're cruising down the highway and parroting the voices of outsiders, which are transmitted to them on the radio. Richman incorporates something of Reed without abandoning himself.

There was a lot of pressure on Richman—a great, eccentric songwriter—to go the way of Reed, to really sing about drugs and darkness. But he didn't want to go in that direction; he was a happy guy, even if he wanted to write like Reed. And Reed, of course, was a really intense, beautiful poet who was dealing with postwar Jewish identity. Think of "Heroin": the beat gets louder and louder, and Reed lets loose a cascade of images, one of which is of "dead bodies piled up in mounds." He didn't have a choice to be a tough guy or not, to be nice or not. As he sings in "Busload of Faith": "You can't depend on the goodly hearted / the goodly hearted made lampshades and soap."

How many of you have studied the Talmud?

OK, for the uninitiated: the Talmud is the book of Jewish law, the guide to daily life; the Torah relays the teachings of G-d as recorded by Moses, the story of the Jewish people. The Talmud is a collection of conversations and questions going back centuries and centuries: on each page, laws that were passed along by mouth thousands of years ago are surrounded by discussions among ancient scholars, commentaries from the Middle Ages, and all the interpretations, cross-references, rulings, explanations, etc. that followed. Talmud study is all about citations and quotations—the questions are never resolved.

I was just looking at Nechama Leibowitz's interpretations of *Ki Tavo*, the portion of the Torah for this week. Have you taken a look at this week's *Parshah*? Are you in my reading group? If not, you're welcome: thousands of Jews around the world dissecting a different passage every Saturday, open and free to all. No buffet, unfortunately, but sometimes there's kiddush with wine and cakes that are sweet as honey and dry as cardboard.

Reading Leibowitz on G-d's endless description of how the Hebrews will suffer if they betray the covenant, I thought about the difference between her scholarship and the kind of articles that I publish as an academic. Forget the codes and conventions of the MLA, forget glosses and footnotes: Leibowitz, like the greatest Torah interpreters, includes entire pages of Maimonides. She quotes the source in context; she doesn't deal in sound bites.

And that's what Jonathan Richman does: he quotes the entire verse of "Sister Ray."

When I read the Talmud, I think of Leibowitz and Richman, music critics and theorists—especially Jacques Derrida, the French philosopher. Who knows Derrida? He was an Algerian Jew who fell in love with grammatology, and came up with deconstruction—which, of course, is one of the main instruments of Talmudic study. Somehow, no one really noticed the connection between the Talmud and Derrida until the very end of his life, when the philosopher Hélène Cixous wrote *Portrait of Jacques Derrida as a Young Jewish Saint*, which is all about Derrida's Jewishness.

Are you with me? This was intended to be parenthetical. (This has all been parenthetical.)

The Talmud was the radio before the radio; the radio of the diaspora. The Talmud, like the radio, binds us together across time and distance, allowing us to imagine identities that transcend Queens circa 1977—the year that I was bar mitzvahed and, supposedly, became a man. And the radio, like the Talmud, provides us with a sense of what Walter Benjamin called "messianic time": the notion that history is unresolved, contingent, and nonlinear. What does that mean? The past and future are alive in the present, and anything can happen at any moment: the dead can be redeemed, the lost revolutions can be won. That's why I've always loved the radio so much. And, I suppose, that's why I've always loved the Talmud so much.

The Talmud was the radio before the radio, and the prophets were rock stars before rock stars. That's why I'm interested in rock stars: you turn on the radio and they give you the word, they give you access to divinity. You believe them because they've been authorized to convey the message. That explains the swagger, I think—and the conjunction of otherworldliness and lucidity that you see in Lou Reed, Patti Smith, Prince, Ian Curtis, and George Clinton. They've been in contact with a higher power! They've wandered through the wilderness, sought the voice of G-d, and witnessed the revelation. The voice of the wilderness speaks through them.

I've always been looking for prophets, and if not for the radio I'd never have found them. Thankfully, I found Lou Reed—and I found Patti Smith.

In the late 1980s, I was desperate for prophets. In my own wandering, I needed hope, I needed a sign. I needed to feel close to the divine. I had Reed, thankfully, and I also had Patti Smith. I thought that Smith, like Reed, was singing to me—singing to those of us in the AIDS movement. She wasn't giving us directives or rules; she was giving us the sense that what we were doing had mystical meaning. Her message:

> I was dreaming in my dreaming
> Of an aspect bright and fair
> And my sleeping, it was broken
> But my dream, it lingered near
>
> In the form of shining valleys
> Where the pure air recognized
> And my senses newly opened
> I awakened to the cry
>
> That the people have the power
> To redeem the work of fools
> Upon the meek the graces shower
> It's decreed: the people rule

To me, the radio was a utopian dream. But by the late 1970s, many performers had turned against the radio, which had gotten too commercial, too much of a mall for music. And that'd made music too homogenous, too much about getting the right product to the right demographic. Patti Smith declared that radio was dead. Musicians wrote songs *for* radio that railed *against* radio. Here's Elvis Costello's "Radio Radio," from 1978:

> I was tuning in the shine on the late night dial
> Doing anything my radio advised
> With every one of those late night stations
> Playing songs bringing tears to my eyes
> I was seriously thinking about hiding the receiver

When the switch broke 'cause it's old
They're saying things that I can hardly believe
They really think we're getting out of control

Radio is a sound salvation
Radio is cleaning up the nation
They say you better listen to the voice of reason
But they don't give you any choice 'cause they think
 that it's treason
So you had better do as you are told
You better listen to the radio

I wanna bite the hand that feeds me
I wanna bite that hand so badly
I want to make them wish they'd never seen me

Some of my friends sit around every evening
And they worry about the times ahead
But everybody else is overwhelmed by indifference
And the promise of an early bed
You either shut up or get cut up; they don't wanna
 hear about it
It's only inches on the reel-to-reel
And the radio is in the hands of such a lot of fools
Tryin' to anesthetize the way that you feel

The radio is a tool of the man: "You had better do as you are told / You better listen to the radio." Radio is commercial, it's all about indoctrination and domination; it's no path to salvation.

I wasn't ready to give up on the radio or accuse DJs of mind control because they were all playing the same Rolling Stones song every forty minutes. I didn't mind the feeling of being at one with the masses. I remember being at the beach on Long Island right after *Emotional Rescue* came out, in 1980, and hearing the title song on someone's radio—muddled and muted at first, mixed with the waves and wind, then, as I got closer, loud and clear. Suddenly, I heard "Emotional Rescue" behind and ahead of me, on three and then thirty radios. Everyone was tuned to the same station. Everyone was turning up the volume. I walked and listened to the entire song. I listened to everyone on the beach listening to the song, separately but together. For five minutes, "Emotional Rescue" was the horizon.

If I'd truly been a punk, I'd have been disgusted by that scene, right? I'd have smashed all the radios with a baseball bat. I'd never have been caught dead on the beach!

The real punks were making radio songs that were critical of the radio. The pinnacle of the anti-radio radio song is "Transmission," by Joy Division, a band that was named after the women in concentration camps who were forced into prostitution and made available to hard-working prisoners. (After Curtis died, the band was rechristened New Order, which was a bit too on the nose.) Ian Curtis and his bandmates weren't fascists, but they were playing fast and loose with Nazi imagery; they were treating symbols of the Holocaust with irony. Why? Well, as Sontag pointed out, the Nazis really did have the best uniforms.

Have you seen Michael Winterbottom's film *24 Hour Party People*? I love the moment when the owner of a club accuses the band members of being Nazis and the manager says, "Have you never heard of Situationism or postmodernism? Do you know about the play of signs and signifiers?"

In "Transmission," Curtis sings about the mechanization of music and bodies, the connection between technologies of transmission and control.

> Radio, live transmission
> Radio, live transmission
>
> Listen to the silence, let it ring on
> Eyes, dark gray lenses frightened of the sun
> We would have a fine time living in the night
> Left to blind destruction
> Waiting for our sight
>
> And we would go on as though nothing was wrong
> And hide from these days we remained all alone
> Staying in the same place, just staying out the time
> Touching from a distance
> Further all the time
>
> Dance, dance, dance, dance, dance to the radio

Fortunately, radio didn't die with Joy Division. Technology changed and salvation arrived in two forms: disco and hip-hop, which emancipated people from the radio via tape cassettes and boom boxes. Suddenly, the party was wherever you were, wherever you wanted the party to be. In LL Cool J's "I Can't Live Without My Radio," the radio turns into a sign of mobility *and* control, a link to on-air DJs *and* a means of bypassing them by switching to the tape deck.

> My radio, believe me, I like it loud
> I'm the man with a box that can rock the crowd
> Walkin' down the street to the hardcore beat
> While my JVC vibrates the concrete
>
> I'm sorry if you can't understand
> But I need a radio inside my hand
> Don't mean to offend other citizens
> But I kick my volume way past 10
>
> My story is rough, my neighborhood is tough
> But I still sport gold and I'm out to crush
> My name is Cool J, I devastate the show
> But I couldn't survive without my radio
>
> ...
>
> Suckers on my jock when I walk down the block
> I really don't care if you're jealous or not
> 'Cause I make the songs, you sing along
> And your radio's def when my record's on
>
> So get off the wall, become involved
> All your radio problems have now been solved

LL Cool J knows that radio hasn't died. The radio has birthed the boombox, a tool of production and transmission that puts the listener in control. You record songs and DJ sets from the radio and from tapes; you make mixtapes and play them for your friends and neighbors, on the street and at parties. Like the turntable, the radio has been reinvented as an instrument, and the technology has taken on a completely new significance—an evangelical significance. The means of transmission have become the medium.

What happened when the turntable became the medium? We went from boulevards to warehouses—and, for me, from speed and coke to ecstasy. I'm sure many of you followed the same trajectory. We danced to the turntable as a medium. We danced to Marshall Jefferson's "Move Your Body."

> Gotta have house music all night long
> With that house music you can't go wrong
>
> Give me that house music to set me free
> Lost in house music is where I wanna be
>
> Move your body

An evangelical moment. Marshall Jefferson had a huge influence on my masculinity: his music—house music—was the soundtrack for worship at gay temple. Move your body, work your body, jack your body—anything you can do with your body.

I used "Move Your Body" for a video I made in 1988 for the Gay Men's Health Crisis about the need for people with AIDS to take care of themselves, to support their immune systems. I wanted everything I was experiencing to pass through me; I was coming home from the clubs and going straight into the editing room.

After the AIDS crisis hit, in 1988, I realized that I might have exposed myself to HIV. I had friends and lovers who were getting sick. And, to put it in plain English, I'd been fucked without a condom many times. I wasn't messing with needles, but I was using a lot of drugs when I went out partying or cruising. Even if I knew better, I wasn't always sober enough to remember—or figure out how—to practice safe sex.

I went to the Lesbian and Gay Community Services Center, on Thirteenth Street, for a consultation. I was living in the East Village, and Chelsea was a completely different culture—a *gay* culture. I was still an anarchist: I didn't want to be gay. I didn't want to be labeled. *You can't put me in a box!* But I had a conversion experience at the Center. I sat down with Denise Ribble, a legendary nurse, and talked about the sex I was having, the drugs I was doing. She was kind and open, and she listened to me without judgment.

I left in tears. I was on the steps of the Center, looking up at the sign, and I thought: *I'm home. I'm going to be gay. I'm going to be part of this community. And I'm going to make a contribution*. I had no idea what the contribution might be! But I knew that I was going to need the community and the community was going to need me—and everyone like me.

After being diagnosed, I had the sense of being compromised, weakened. At the same time, I came to understand myself as a queer man, and as part of a community to which I was indebted. I realized the importance of having an identity—or *choosing* an identity. I moved to Chelsea, which was the only neighborhood where you could walk around looking as sick as I did without anyone looking askance at you. Being sick was normal. I remember sitting at a restaurant and seeing someone throw up on his plate. The waitstaff rolled with it. Everyone rolled with it.

Somehow, I survived for long enough to get on protease inhibitors. But from the moment I was diagnosed until 1996, when I got on medication, my life was shaped by the notion that I had no time. I was never far from death.

I had no time. So I was listening to "Born to Lose," by the Heartbreakers. Do you know the song? It's the American equivalent of the Sex Pistols' "No Future."

When there's no future, how can there be sin?
We're the flowers in the dustbin
We're the poison in your human machine
We're the future
Your future

Actually, I take that back: "No Future" is the English equivalent to "Born to Lose." Anyone—Johnny Thunders? He was from Queens, too, but not a Jew. I relate to him in part because, as a teenager, I was a Juido. You know what a Juido is, right? A Jew who looks like an Italian—a species commonly found in Long Island. I had a gold chain with a horn and long hair like Travolta's, parted in the middle, complete with feathers.

Johnny Thunders—born as John Anthony Genzale—was a wreck. He was very flamboyant; he always wore a captain's hat. Often, he was so messed up that he could barely walk onto the stage. But when he played, he'd get hundreds of kids to sing along.

That's the way it goes
This city is so cold
And I'm—I'm so sold
That's why I know
I said hit it

Born to lose
Born to lose
Born to lose
Oh, baby, I'm born to lose

> Oh, nothing to do
> Oh, nothing to say
> Only one thing that I want
> It's the only way
> I said hit it

I loved Johnny Thunders. In retrospect, though, I wonder what drives a kid to idealize a heroin addict. I don't know. There's something to the complete commitment to pleasure and the refusal to perform competence, which is what the straight world expects. And there's honesty in Thunders's admission. If you're born to lose, there's no point in playing the game; there's no point in pretending that your place in society will change if you professionalize, wear a suit, and move to the suburbs.

I don't want to go back on drugs, but I'm holding on to that sense of being an underdog, a loser. I'm still embracing Thunders's admission as a position—a punk political position. For me, learning to embrace that position meant understanding myself in relation to oppressed people, and fighting with them. What else can you do if you've got no time, no future? How else can you find freedom?

One thing you can do, I suppose, is retreat from the world—or create a world apart from the one that's defined you as a loser, an outsider, a threat, a reprobate, a vector of disease. That's what punk musicians like Johnny Thunders were doing, and that's why hundreds of kids were singing along: they wanted another world. They wanted a future that was nothing like the world of their parents—nothing like the *real* world, the *straight* world, the *natural* world.

I didn't want anything to do with the real world. I wasn't fighting to be accepted; I was fighting for the rights of people who *weren't* going to be accepted. I was fighting for people who didn't want to pass, people who didn't want to be patted on the back for being normal. My position was a queer position: if being queer is unnatural, then I'm against nature. I choose being who I am, not being part of a world that's built on the exclusion of people like me.

This queer position has a long history, of course. I always go back to Joris-Karl Huysmans's 1884 novel *À rebours*, which translates as "against nature" or "against the grain." Huysmans writes about a wealthy Parisian libertine who retires to the countryside after getting sick of his lifestyle and society. Having rejected the world, he devotes himself to creating increasingly surreal alternatives in the rooms of his mansion: he plants a garden of poisonous tropical flowers that resemble fake ones; he covers the shell of a tortoise with gemstones that match his Persian rug, crushing the animal. He decides to visit London after reading Dickens, but turns around after realizing that he'd only be disappointed by the real city, the real people, the real tastes and smells.

To me, *À rebours* is about what to do with the feeling of alienation and marginalization. When reality is a nightmare, you have to come up with an alternative, right? You have to turn to artifice. You have to *envision* another world in order to *make* that world. And that's what Huysmans and the other Decadents were after: a world of and for art and beauty—a world away from the moralism and scientism of the Victorian era.

For a while, I really couldn't get with the Decadents. To me, the movement seemed like an amplification of Romanticism, except the Decadents found salvation in aesthetics rather than nature. That, at least, made sense to me, having grown up in Queens: Grand Central Parkway and Flushing Meadows Park were as close as I got to nature, and I was *not* inspired. I shared the objection to rationalism and wage slavery, but I'd been trained to be anti-aesthetics, to be on the side of the Bauhaus and Minimalism. So I had a hard time with the revival of Romanticism in the 1980s, especially among queer people. Everyone was watching Derek Jarman films and going to the opera. And the movies and books about AIDS were all about humanizing gay men through accounts of love and loss, intimacy and suffering.

Have you read Paul Monette's *Borrowed Time*? It's a memoir of his partner—handsome, affluent, connected, a member of the Los Angeles elite—dying of AIDS and working his way into experimental drug trials. What about Norman René's *Longtime Companion*? It's the first mainstream movie about AIDS: predictably, the characters are relatable, successful, well-to-do friends whose lives are upended by the disease, and who find solace in loving relationships.

At the time, my thought was: enough with all the star-crossed lovers finding beauty in dying together! Enough with the *Liebestod*!

Liebestod, of course, is the name of the final piece from Wagner's *Tristan und Isolde*. And it's a brilliant German contraction: "love death," or the consummation of love in death. You remember how Brontë's Heathcliff bangs his head against the tree upon the moor, refuses food, and wills himself to die so that he can join his beloved Catherine in the afterlife, right? That's another Liebestod, another Romantic vision of souls merging in death. Much better than "till death do us part," right? Much better than collecting the deceased's social security checks.

I'd been taught that Romanticism is indulgent, aristocratic, asocial, immoral. And, after me and my friends began to get sick—after we began to care for, lose, and mourn our lovers—I had even less patience for the fantasy of the Liebestod. I couldn't find anything beautiful about what we were experiencing. And, as far as I could tell, neither could anyone else who'd gone through what we were going through. I couldn't understand what dying from AIDS had to do with consummating love, much less submitting to nature or perfecting the spirit.

Then I started going to the opera. Some friends who were great opera queens took me to Wagner's *Die Walküre*, the apogee of Romanticism. Watching the psychodrama of the Norse gods, I realized that Romanticism is pretty appealing as a response to the Enlightenment and the industrial revolution. I mean, if you set aside the Teutonic nationalism and anti-Semitism, you've got a powerful argument against life being all about reason and order, and people being treated as—or replaced by—machines.

I started to appreciate that the Romantics had thought of art as picking up where religion had left off. Wagner's *Ring Cycle* is art as religion—or, at least, art as a substitute for religion. He responds to the death of G-d by creating new myths, reviving spirituality through aesthetics. His operas are antidotes to the disenchantment of the modern world. They counter heartless rationalism and soul-sucking industrialism with journeys into "the primordial chaos of human nature," in Friedrich Schlegel's words.

What I'm trying to say is: my first opera was *Die Walküre*! Pretty macho, huh? I'm proud to say that I didn't start with Puccini or Verdi.

[*Sings a few lines from Verdi's* Chorus of the Hebrew Slaves.]

No, no, no—*Die Walküre*!

I became a Wagner convert, and I never stopped listening to Iggy Pop. Gradually, I came to understand the punk position as encompassing the Romantic position, the Decadent position, and the queer position. Plus prophesy! Iggy took me to another world: a world of revelation and reinvention. He wasn't ashamed to be sick, strung out, born to lose, abnormal. He'd gone to the wilderness and come back as a free person—with mascara and lipstick. Look at the cover of *Raw Power*: Iggy is sick and free.

I'm thinking of Iggy's song "Beyond the Law." He articulates the feeling of being so disregarded, so excluded from the social bargain, that your concerns aren't relevant to everyone else's. Your existence has nothing to do with theirs, and vice versa.

We don't do what we're supposed to, see?
We got no manners anyway
There's danger in our honesty
'Cause trouble comes to those who are free

Can anybody hear me when I call?
The real scene is out beyond the law

Some people say we're negative
They say we take and never give
They say our lives are a mistake
But the truth is in the sound we make

Can anybody hear me when I call?
The real scene is out beyond the law

We don't believe in anything, we don't stand for nothing
We got no V for victory, 'cause we know things are tougher

We don't believe in anything, we don't stand for nothing
We got no V for victory, 'cause we know things are tougher

The straights all hate the sound we make
Because they know their walls will shake
So when they say our vibes are bad
They're running scared and looking sad

"We don't stand for nothing." Same position as Johnny Thunders. Being beyond the law is like being born to lose. Being an outsider is like being a drug addict: at a certain point, whether you're a Republican or Democrat, all that matters is how you're going to get your next fix.

Recently, I've felt closer to Iggy Pop and Johnny Thunders's position than I have in a long time, since before I tested positive. I've felt the familiar despair and disaffection. "We've got no V for victory, 'cause we know things are tougher," right? We know things are tougher because we're dealing with problems that aren't part of straight life, and that have to do with being shut out of straight life. And no matter what we do, we have to keep asking: "Can anyone hear me when I call?"

On the other hand, we can hear each other—and we can hear our prophets. We've got no future, but we've got the truth in the sound we make; we've got the power to make walls shake. Which means we have a future.

That's what I'm after: a future. Not laughs. A future.

[*Applause.*]

Chapter 2: The Rabbi

Hello! Welcome to the *Benyamin Zev Show.* Benyamin Zev is my Hebrew name, if you don't know. If I'm called on to read the Torah at temple, which is an honor, I'm called Benyamin Zev; if my name is inscribed in the Book of Life, the name will be Benyamin Zev. How'd I get the name? Well, you might have guessed that I was circumcised. Usually, when you're brought into the covenant, you're given a Hebrew name that's an approximation of your English name: Moses is Moshe, Samuel is Shmuel, and so on. But I was named Benyamin Zev. Why? To honor a relative of my mother's, someone I've never met and know nothing about.

In other words, on the eighth day of my life I became Benyamin Zev *and* Gregg Bordowitz. Benyamin isn't derived from Gregg; Zev doesn't stand for Bordowitz.

I've always been interested in names—G-d's name, especially, but also my own. It's not quite as rich as a topic, but it's easier to pronounce. And there's no taboo on saying Gregg! I'm not allowed to say G-d's name. Only the high priest of the First Temple in Jerusalem was permitted to say G-d's four-letter name—the "ineffable name," the "unutterable name." Then, after the Romans sieged Jerusalem and destroyed the Second Temple, pronouncing the word was forbidden.

The past two thousand years have been rough for Jews. We've gotten to be somewhat anxious; we've learned to keep secrets. Religious Jews have taken great care to conceal the true name of G-d, in order to prevent that which is most holy from being profaned. You can't curse our god if you don't know the name, right? But concealing the name also means distinguishing between *divinity* and the *aspects* of divinity as we describe them, which are representations of something that can't really be represented. Instead of pronouncing G-d's name, we refer to the four letters as the Tetragrammaton.

Actually, there are a number of names for G-d in the Bible, and various times and places when you're supposed to use or avoid them. Given the secular circumstances, the word I'll use tonight is Hashem, which means "the name." Another name for—or aspect of—G-d is Shechinah. How many of you felt the presence of the Shechinah today?

One? We've got a witness. One blessed person. For those who don't know, the Shechinah is the female manifestation, or principle, of G-d, and dwells among the mortals. The Sabbath is her day. Every Saturday, those who're observant—and some who aren't—await the Shechinah.

I felt the Shechinah visit today. I had some peace. And I had some Klonopin.

A lot of *zaddiks* in the room tonight! Welcome! I hope you all had a good Shabbos. I hope you had some ... peace. And the same to those of you who're lacking in righteousness: Gregg David Bordowitz welcomes you.

[*Audience applauds.*]

Thank you, thank you. I have to ask, though: Who are you applauding? Who is ... *Gregg*?

Gregg is the result of assimilation and divorce. I was born Gregg David Harstein; I got my biological father's last name. But he left us when I was four, and my mother married Martin—or Moshe, same as Moses—Bordowitz. He adopted me and we adopted his name.

I admit that I never really identified with my given name. I feel more like Benyamin Zev. Benyamin means son of the south, or son of the right hand, and Zev means wolf—I'm inheriting and I'm howling. Pretty good, right? Gregg, however, is a tall, thin, blonde guy somewhere in Connecticut, wearing pink tennis shorts, drinking a gin and tonic. And David? If I were Christian, I'd have gotten a middle name when I was christened; I'm Jewish, though, so I wasn't christened (as far as I know), and yet I have a middle name.

Why? Well ... I'm American. Why else?

My mother wanted me to have a *real* American name, I guess. Why not David at school and Dovid at shul? I don't know. She chose Gregg, even though—or because—she didn't like Gregory. Too many syllables. The two *g*'s in Gregg are emphatic: the second one is to make sure no one calls me Gregory.

I grew up with kids who were given similar American names for similar reasons. Randall Lautenberg, my childhood best friend: that's the name of a royal, so Randall was bound to be a letdown. He did what he could, though; he was a fine Jewish boy.

My mom's maiden name is Linda Bonnie Glassman. Before her family emigrated to the United States, they'd been called Allesman, which means "every man" in Yiddish. It's a funny, fitting switch: from commoner to immigrant, from every man to transparent man. I'm surprised that all Jews weren't renamed Glassman when they got to Ellis Island!

Here's an Ellis Island joke—a rabbi joke: a Jew from Eastern Europe lands at Ellis Island, having fled from poverty, pogroms, and a low-calorie diet. He's exhausted, confused, overwhelmed. He's hardly able to figure out where to stand in line, much less how to explain himself. Finally, he approaches a counter and an official asks for his name. He replies, "*Shayn fergessen*," which, in Yiddish, means "I've already forgotten." His new name? Sean Ferguson.

Actually, the story about people like my mother's parents changing their names at Ellis Island is a myth. Alan Berliner made a great film about this, *The Sweetest Sound*. He found that there were plenty of translators at Ellis Island during the greatest wave of Jewish immigration, from the late 1800s to the early 1900s. The names weren't changed by the government. They were changed by the immigrants, most of whom were carrying documents printed with their names. The Jews were ashamed; they wanted to discard the past. They didn't just arrive and say, "Hey, I'd like to be an American. Steve? Sure. The past two thousand years *have* been rough for Jews..."

Half of my stepfather's family changed their name from Bordowitz to Bordo, like Bordeaux, as in ... French. As in French wine. *Grand cru*.

Names are important to me. Since my Hebrew name means "wolf," I got a wolf logo for the set.

[*Points to a sign, hanging from the curtain behind him, with a silhouette of a howling wolf.*]

A close friend reminded me that the sign looks a lot like the logo for the Badlands, a gay bar in the West Village that I used to go to in the early '80s. Anyone remember the Badlands? One time, I was standing outside and I saw a cab pull up: two guys in full leather motorcycle gear got out, carrying helmets under their arms. They walked past me, into the Badlands, and put their helmets on the bar, as if they'd just hopped off their hogs. I was in awe. That's when I realized—and came to admire—the amount of artifice involved in fetishes.

Anyway, I had some fine moments at the Badlands. I'd been fascinated by the West Village since I was in high school, when a guidance counselor took pity on me because I was being bullied. He recognized me as queer and he came out to me; he asked if I wanted to go the city. Honestly, I thought we were going to a museum—an edifying field trip for a kid with a mild case of alienation. But he took me to a leather shop on Christopher Street and I bought a leather hat with metal studs. What a guidance counselor!

When I was leaving high school, the counselor said, "So, you're going to New York. You're going to hear rumors of what people are calling gay cancer. I just want to tell you that you can't get cancer from sex." He was right—and, of course, terribly wrong. At that point, though, no one understood why men who have sex with men were contracting a novel STD. The disease wasn't associated with gay men until 1982, when the CDC released a report on "gay-related immune deficiency," or GRID, a misnomer that set so much violent homophobia in motion.

Names, again.

The guidance counselor, Randall Lautenberg, Linda Bonnie Glassman, Sean Ferguson, the "ineffable name"—they delivered me, Benyamin Zev, to you. They prepared me to wander. And, as such, I wanted the set to bring them together—or to bring *me* together. I wanted the set to have a wandering-Jew-unpacking-his-library feel.

[*Points to the books and other objects on shelves on the stage.*]

These beloved books constitute my research for the show. And, I suppose, they constitute myself: the Talmud (English, Hebrew, and Aramaic), Moses ben Jacob Cordovero's *Or Ne'erav*, Hannah Arendt's *Eichmann in Jerusalem*, Nehama Leibowitz's *New Studies in Shemot*, Abraham Joshua Heschel's *God in Search of Man*, the Berkeley feminist Haggadah, Daniel Boyarin's *Unheroic Conduct: The Rise of Heterosexuality and the Invention of the Jewish Man*, and on and on.

You can't wait for the footnotes, right?

I don't own this stage, but I want you to feel like I do, like you're trapped inside my head. Like you're ... me.

[*Walks to the table on stage and picks up object after object.*]

I've got my siddur, my kiddush cup, and my tallit bag, which I take to shul. And, since it's almost *yontif*, I've got the setup: kosher salt, apples, colander, honey, challah, and a challah cover. I had someone go through a great deal of trouble to get a wooden meat tenderizer. To be honest, I'm not sure why I need a meat tenderizer; I guess I'm experiencing a high level of anxiety and I find comfort in the prospect of tenderizing. Or maybe I'm the meat?

[*Gently pounds his open palm with the meat tenderizer.*]

Are any of you shomer Shabbos? I guess not; if you were, you wouldn't be here, though perhaps you're transgressing for the occasion? Don't worry, you're good, you're good—so long as you're not carrying money, you went to shul, and you've read *Pirkei Avot*.

I'm not shomer Shabbos, obviously. I'm here. I even have my phone on. (Don't worry, it's on silent.) I need my phone: I have all seventy volumes of the Babylonian Talmud in my hand!

[*Triumphantly hoists up the phone with his right hand.*]

Watch out: the Jews are in cyberspace! We're everywhere.

[*Points to the phone with his left hand.*]

Last night, I was a rock star; tonight, I'm a rabbi. Last night, we sang along with Lou Reed at the Bottom Line, we pogoed to the Ramones at CBGB, and we sweated to Marshall Jefferson at the Roxy.

Tonight ... don't feel bad! Tonight's different, but good. Tonight, we're going to temple; we're going to *daven*.

The rabbi isn't so different from the rock star, really! That's what I tell myself, at least. I like to think of the rock star as a storyteller, a maggid—a preacher who travels the land telling tales—and not a rabbi with a congregation, a parking spot, and a 401(k). The standard rabbi shows up at temple and lectures on a passage from the Bible, but the maggid begins to preach by responding to questions asked by the people.

A rock star like Lou Reed shows up in your town, takes the stage, and tells a story. He performs a song like "Walk on the Wild Side," which isn't so different from a Torah story: a tale with an ethical dimension. But the meaning of a song—whether a story is being told or not—also has to do with the event of the performance, the manner in which the song is sung, the relationship between the performer and the audience, the time and place. The song is the event; the narration and interpretation are as important as the words, and the point of the words is to produce endless narrations and interpretations. That's one way to understand rock and roll, and it's also one way to understand Jewish liturgy.

What am I doing tonight? I'm demonstrating my

formula: some rock stars are rabbis, some rabbis are rock stars—and both are comedians.

What else? I'm trying to learn something. I'm thinking about the corpus of Jewish thought, the discussions and disagreements that have been going on for thousands of years. I'm asking how I went from getting bar mitzvahed at Young Israel, a Modern Orthodox Jewish temple in New Hyde Park, to occupying government offices to protest the inhuman response to the AIDS crisis, to performing my ethnicity on stage. I'm looking to *Queer Theory and the Jewish Question*, which says there's something queer about being a Jew and something racy about being a queer. I'm trying to figure out how I came to understand my ethnicity in relation to my gender, sexuality, nation, and race—and my identity as impossible to reduce to any of those categories. I'm wondering why so many Americans, with such various backgrounds and experiences, have embraced a national identity that pits them against people who are different (or more different, or more recently different)—and hinges on patriarchy, racial domination, xenophobia, and conquest. I'm digging into the history of Jewish life and thought—the exodus to Queens, the never-ending commentaries on the same old books—in order to find an alternative: an identity that accounts for all aspects of ourselves and how they impinge on each other.

"Good luck," some of you are saying. I heard it—I know you didn't say it out loud, but I heard it! "Good luck." Or, "*Gai kakken*." That means, "Go take a shit"—a Yiddish curse that often comes in handy. My grandmother taught me that one. She used to tell me to go take a shit all the time.

My grandparents' families arrived at Ellis Island at the beginning of the twentieth century. They came to the US along with tens of thousands of Russian Jews who were under attack after being blamed for the assassination of the tsar, the death of Jesus, and whatever misfortunes the locals had endured. They had good reason to call themselves Steve! Or Bordo.

I have six grandparents, including my stepfather's parents, and they were all born to immigrants on the Lower East Side. My mother's father, Max Glassman, grew up in a tenement on Avenue A and Fifth Street, and pushed me to become a rabbi from the time I was a child. I liked to read, I didn't play sports—what do you expect?

I didn't have too many options for positive role models who identified as Jewish. The stories I used to hear: anyone who was famous, successful, and embraced being Jewish—or was even recognizable as Jewish—stood in for *the* Jews. Einstein was Jewish: *You could be a scientist!* Henry Kissinger was

Jewish: *You could be a warmonger!* Otherwise ... lawyers, doctors, and rabbis, in that order.

I grew up in a Yiddish household, and I went to a grade school in Queens that was closed for all high holidays. My teachers encouraged me by revealing that Bob Dylan's real name was Robert Zimmerman. *You could be a rock star!* Dylan, of course, was not a typical rock star: he had a nasal whine, a big nose, and a Jewfro. He was more of a rabbi, really.

I could've been a rabbi. Eventually, though, I became a teenager. My parents felt like they had fulfilled their obligation to my grandfather, and they were sick of driving me to temple. I moved on. I went to Christopher Street, I went to CBGB. Nevertheless, I've always thought of myself as a rabbi in training—or as a candidate for retraining. I've always thought of the rabbi as a model for being a man, an American, and a Jew.

I'm not saying I subscribe to the model, though. When I was a teenager, I tried to drain my speech of the Brooklyn Jew accent, the Yiddish inflections, the wetness. How'd that work? Well, I'm fifty-four, and I'm still trying, even though I've turned my ethnicity into a career. Or perhaps I've realized that I've always been on stage, I've always been playing—or desperately playing against—a role. I mean: look at me, listen to me!

I do have *some* sense of how others perceive me. I've been attuned to how people look at me, how they talk to me, and how they laugh at me—or … *with* me?—for quite a while. And how've I responded? Sometimes I've embodied the stereotype, cranked up the wetness; sometimes I've confronted bigotry, told the homophobic anti-Semites what's what; and sometimes I've been overwhelmed with anxiety and shame. Even at my age, I have fears of being … *too* Jewish.

You know what that means, right? Eating too much at the buffet, standing too close to other people—especially at the buffet. Sharing too many opinions, asking too many questions, ending every sentence with a question mark. Wearing loud clothing, unfashionable clothing, ill-fitting clothing.

I'm guilty on all counts. I was dressed by my mom. Or I dressed myself like she dressed me—when she wasn't dressing me.

I'll bring this up with my therapist, I suppose.

[*Indistinct question from the audience about attire and self-expression.*]

What did I wear? Why? What was the offense? I wore a Qiana shirt! You remember Qiana shirts? Polyester, meant to look like silk; geometric, psychedelic patterns; enormous collars; available at Sears. I wore them open to halfway down my hairless chest, my mane falling against the collar. (My mother let me grow my hair as long as I wanted.) I matched the shirts with big leather belts, bell bottoms, and—my favorite—a leather vest with fringes, which had been my dad's and was the only item of value that my mom got in the divorce, I believe. What else? Earth Shoes. The sole was thinner at the heel than at the toe, so you felt like you were walking up a hill—"negative heel technology." The shoes were supposed to bounce you along.

As you can guess, I was mercilessly teased at school. My neighborhood was not the type where everyone appreciated such sartorial choices. When I showed up to Hebrew school, I quickly went to the bathroom, took off my Qiana shirt and vest, put on my tzitzit, made sure the strings were hanging out, rummaged through my bag to find my kippah, and ran to class.

My choice in clothing has improved, I guess, but sometimes I look in the mirror and worry about how much I resemble myself as a twelve-year-old on the way to Hebrew school.

[*Looks down and tugs at the lapels of his suit jacket, fiddles with his necktie, tugs at the cuffs of his white dress shirt.*]

My parents were Jewish working-class hippies, and they wanted nothing to do with Hebrew school.

Max, my mother's father, was raised Orthodox; he wanted his first grandson to have a religious education. He wanted me to study Talmud and be bar mitzvahed at an Orthodox temple. And that's what he got, because he was paying the tuition. Eventually, my parents saw the benefits. "Well, it's an after-school activity," they thought. "And he's not about to become Sandy Koufax. So he'll have something to do—and he'll come home late four days a week for four years!"

Hebrew school is the equivalent of graduate school: I knew the difference between deductive and inductive reasoning when I was eleven years old. I don't have a college degree, but I do have Guttman's *Philosophies of Judaism*, Ganzfried's *Code of Jewish Law*, and Landau's *The Life and Teachings of Rabbi Eliyahu the Gaon of Vilna*. I don't have an investment portfolio, but I do have a library that takes up half my apartment, which means I get a tax deduction.

I usually went to shul alone. Sometimes my grandfather came with me, but he had trouble walking into the temple. The war ruined religion for him. Maybe I was supposed to help him heal. Maybe I was supposed to bring him back to G-d, who'd abandoned him. For a while, at least, I was on the path: I was going to take on the burden of redeeming the suffering of my forebears and renewing the collective faith. I was going to re-enchant the world.

The chief rabbi of our synagogue was Rabbi Bilitski, who was Orthodox—not modern Orthodox, but Haredi. He had a long white beard and fingertips that were stained yellow from chain-smoking. He was a corpulent man with tiny, soft hands; he obviously had never done physical labor, though he might have occasionally gotten a paper cut. I often sat and talked to Rabbi Bilitski in his basement office while he smoked cigarette after cigarette, whether because I had a question about the Torah or because I'd said something offensive in class. Both were frequent occurrences.

One day, when I was with Rabbi Bilitski in his office, he told me I was going to be a rabbi. I was honored! He told my parents I'd make a great rabbi. And they probably thought, "Well, how much is that going to cost?" We often had trouble paying the tuition, which was embarrassing. None of the other families had issues coming up with the money. My grandfather would give us part of the tuition and we'd ask to pay the rest later, as if we were dealing with the mafia. But I was never made to feel unwelcome; I was never barred from shul until I paid up.

In fact, after Rabbi Bilitski encouraged me to become a rabbi, he invited me to Shabbos at his house. My stepfather walked me over and Rabbi Bilitski didn't invite him in; clearly, there'd been some kind of negotiation in advance and he wasn't going to cross the threshold. I sat across from the rabbi's son, Yitzhak, who was slightly older than me—much larger than me—and wearing a three-piece suit with a black fedora. They wanted to show me what a real Shabbos dinner was like. They wanted to show me, I think, what it'd be like if I weren't the kid whose parents keep the engine running while they drop him off at shul, if I weren't the kid who puts on his kippah and tzitzit in the bathroom before class.

When I was eleven, I came under the influence of Rabbi Gordon, who prepared me for my bar mitzvah. Rabbi Gordon was in his mid-to-late twenties, and he already had several kids. He was handsome—very handsome—with olive skin and curly hair: not enough hair to count as a Jewfro, but definitely kinky. He had beautiful hands with muscular, square fingers, like my grandfather's. Extremely clean nails.

What? There's a lot of pointing in Hebrew school!

[*Points at the audience, the stage, the ceiling, the Torah.*]

Rabbi Gordon was really something. He was cool. And ... I was in love with him, obviously. *Come on*!

The synagogue separated the genders, and only the

boys got to daven with the rabbis. You'd open up a siddur or Talmud and you'd see beard hairs on every page. Even as a thirteen-year-old, I had a nascent sense of myself as a feminist, and I knew the entire situation was patriarchal and wrong. The idea is to not be distracted or think about sex, but the smell of dozens of men in heavy clothing, packed into a poorly ventilated room, sweating as they pore over leather-bound scripture, is ... *really* distracting to some people. But I guess the smell of body odor and books is also a powerful pedagogical tool for people like me: people who are ... who like to ... read.

I looked up to rabbis; I thought of myself as a rabbi in training. I imagined my body odor permeating the shul, my beard fusing with the holy books. Does that still happen? Do boys take cues from rabbis? You've got to tell me! I'm not a pre-teen anymore—never mind my outfit—and I haven't had the privilege of raising one.

Who's teaching boys to be men? Tom Brady? Justin Timberlake? I don't know! Let's just say I'm very grateful for the Orthodox rabbis. They taught me to keep my nails clean. And to mark sacred spaces with my sweat.

Rabbi Gordon enlightened me, which is a virtue that I especially appreciate in others. He introduced me to Nehama Leibowitz, an Orthodox Jew and one of the greatest Bible commentators of the twentieth century. For my bar mitzvah, Rabbi Gordon gave me her interpretation of the book of Exodus, *Studies in Shemot*. He said, "Leibowitz is amazing, you have to read her. And she'll take your phone calls! Not only can you write to Nehama Leibowitz, you can call her." I was floored—and very confused. Rabbi Gordon went on: "She lives in Israel, but you can call her anytime, day or night, if you have a question about the Torah. She will answer."

I was twelve years old. I was hardly allowed to call New Jersey, much less my grandparents in Florida. Our avocado-colored phone was attached to the wall, connected with a long spiral cord, and as soon as my mother heard me unhook the handset, she'd get nervous. After two minutes of talking with my grandparents, she'd start tugging on my arm, begging me to get off. "It's long distance, it's long distance!"

How much would calling Israel have cost? How would I have called Israel? How would I have looked up Nehama Leibowitz's phone number? If I'd managed to get her on the line, what would I have asked? I forgot to ask Rabbi Gordon all these questions.

Leibowitz never became a rabbi, because women couldn't be Orthodox rabbis. But she belongs to a tradition of women—many of them daughters of rabbis—who were renowned interpreters of the scripture. And Leibowitz had the entire diaspora as her congregation, so she didn't really need a temple. She was a committed Zionist and, in her twenties, before World War II, she emigrated from Germany to Israel, where she lived for the rest of her life. While teaching at local universities, she advocated for a much more expansive vision of Jewish learning: she revived classic commentaries on the Bible that'd been dropped by yeshivas and secular scholars, including works by non-Orthodox Jews and gentiles, which got her into trouble. Rather than push a point of view, she focused on the meaning of the scripture. She adopted a method of close reading that was connected to New Criticism, which was emerging around the same time in the United States.

In other words, she was a revolutionary! And, like any respectable revolutionary, she cultivated a following. Outside of class, she circulated worksheets for students, asking them to respond to rare and unpublished commentaries, many of them focused on the weekly *parashah*. The students sent the worksheets back to her to correct, and they also told friends and family, who told friends and family. Soon Leibowitz had a global network of thousands of students, connected by the mail. She got a nickname: the queen of questions. She even had a catchphrase: "What's Rashi's difficulty?"

Do you know Rashi?

Rashi—known by one name, like Madonna—was a great medieval French rabbi and Talmud scholar. Leibowitz, however, used him as a stand-in for whichever commentator was under scrutiny. Instead of identifying solutions, she searched for the questions embedded in each verse of scripture: the questions that hadn't been answered by the commentator; the questions that had yet to be asked.

To Leibowitz, the point of religious study isn't to come up with answers. The point is to recognize and ask about whatever you don't understand. But she was far from heretical: she upheld aspects of patriarchy in Judaism as the will of G-d, and she resisted what she saw as the intrusion of secular feminism into religious life. Still, she helped me understand the terrain I was navigating as a prepubescent protofeminist being cultivated by men who looked like they came from the sixteenth century. She helped me understand how tradition holds people together no matter where and how they live, no matter how free they are to reject the world of their ancestors—or their rabbis. She helped me understand that I could wear my leather vest *and* my tzitzit. Theoretically. Eventually. Assuming my sense of style didn't evolve.

Now I've gone from Leibowitz to Rabbi Miriam Grossman, the rabbi at my shul in Brooklyn, Kolot Chayeinu. She replaced Rabbi Ellen Lippmann, who founded Kolot—a brilliant mind and an out lesbian. Obviously, it's not the temple of my bar mitzvah. That said, despite the attachment to segregating the genders, Judaism has never been all about strong men dominating and weak women submitting. Historically, Jewish communities in Europe were often less rigid, or less regressive and domineering, than those of Christians. If you look at the role of gender during the period of *embourgeoisement*—a word I really like to say—in Europe in the 1700s, there's a dissonance between Jews and everyone else. Basically, the women took on the standard responsibilities of men. And the men? They were *feminized*. They studied all day and their wives worked as merchants to support them. That's the source of anti-Semitic myths about Jewish men being effete, queer, or castrated.

I know, I know: on stage tonight, two out of three are true! Generally, though, it's more complicated. Men were prized, even fetishized, and the idea was for them to study while women held down the house and handled the finances. This was the typical Jewish family formation, even before the emergence of the bourgeoisie in Europe, before the merchants began to challenge the power of the landed gentry. Jewish women had more freedom, or latitude, than their Christian counterparts.

Have any of you read *The Memoirs of Glückel of Hameln*?

It's great, especially if you have a soft spot for seventeenth-century diaries of German Jewish widows. Glückel was an Orthodox Jew but also a merchant: she had fourteen children, ran a factory, traveled far and wide to promote her business, and met all kinds of people, who told her about plague, piracy, murder, bankruptcy, war, and false messiahs. Her husband stayed at home, studied, then died.

I highly recommend Glückel's memoirs, which cover her finances as well as her life. And I highly recommend Klonopin.

By the way, I don't get kickbacks from sales of the books, pharmaceuticals, or other products that I recommend. But if there are any publishers in the audience who are interested in the books I *might* mention in my next performance, I'm happy to have a discussion. Same goes for Klonopin: if there are any employees of Genentech in the audience, I'm happy to have a discussion. I'm willing to consider working Klonopin into my next performance—and the one after, and the one after.

OK, I admit it: I already work Klonopin into every performance—one before I get on stage, a few more when I get off. (I call them mints.)

Back to the 1700s: Jews in Europe were merchants because they weren't allowed to do much else. But being a merchant was fairly sexy: you got to escape your husband, your family; you got to see foreign countries and eat foreign food. You didn't get a feminist transformation of gender roles, but you got some relief from the patriarchy, at least.

What happened as a result? In addition to Jewish men being thought of as emasculated, Jewish women were accused of being controlling, bossy, and strong—masculine. In *Unheroic Conduct*, Daniel Boyarin describes the anti-Semitism that went along with the rise of bourgeois society and the corresponding gender roles. Christians didn't approve of the Jewish notion of femininity. They thought the marketplace was for men, and Jews thought the marketplace was for women.

In some neighborhoods in New York, not much has changed: head over to the Hasidic neighborhood in Crown Heights, where I live, or in Williamsburg, and you'll see men going to and from temple, dressed in finery—silk pants and fur hats. The men are peacocks! Where are the women? At home, crunching numbers, staring at spreadsheets—and tending to children. And if you go to Israel, you'll see the distinctiveness of gender roles reflected on billboards, magazine covers, and TV commercials, which tend to feature half-naked men. The advertisements that objectify women in the United States are the same in Israel, more or less, except the men are the airbrushed fetish objects.

I'm not saying that Israelis—or Jews—are like this or that. People don't have an essence that can be reduced to one aspect of identity, whether gender, religion, or race. The idea that they *do* have such an essence is what's behind the ethnonationalist movement in Israel, which I oppose. And it's the idea behind the ethnonationalist movement in the United States, which is the reason why I'm on stage right now.

You think I'm doing this for fun? For fame, money, adulation? Not quite, not yet. I'm here because, in the summer of 2017, I was shocked and horrified to watch white nationalists and neo-Nazis in Charlottesville carry torches and chant, "Jews will not replace us!" I'm here because they threatened, attacked, and killed people like me—people like *us*—based on the belief that Black and brown people are taking what belongs to them, and Jews are orchestrating the plot. I'm here because of the merging of anti-Semitism and racism, because anti-Semitism *is* racism. I'm here because *The Protocols of the Elders of Zion* is trending on Twitter and selling on eBay.

When I saw the Charlottesville rally, I thought about the history of Jewish marginalization and assimilation, and I thought about the choices we make: to cling to our privilege or march with the oppressed; to identify with a nation or a people in diaspora. What did I decide to do? *Schmear* myself in *schmaltz* and grease up the fucking world. After all, my response to stigma has always been to say, "Yes, and..."—which is also the first rule of improv comedy. When I used to get harassed at AIDS rallies by homophobic counter-protesters, I'd say, "Yes, I'm a disgusting faggot, and it's so much worse than you can even imagine! Let me tell you about what we *really* do when we're fucking."

As an activist and a Jew, I want to insist on difference; I don't want to belong to a nation where everyone has equal rights because everyone is the same. Zionists might say that a nation was promised by G-d to the Jews, but when you read about Israel in the Bible or Torah, you're not reading about a nation. You're definitely not reading about the nation-state that now exists in the same territory as another state, Palestine—or even the homeland that's also claimed by another people, the Palestinians. Israel refers to a people in diaspora. In fact, the form of the Talmud backs up this definition: there are two versions, the Babylonian Talmud and the Jerusalem Talmud, because the religion has evolved through debates among Jews in the diaspora. They didn't have email or Google Docs, so they ended up with different bodies of interpretation.

You can even hear the diaspora in the different pronunciations of Torah. *TOY-rah* is Yiddish: wet, phlegmy. *Toe-ruh* is Hebrew: dry, clean. "Tell some *TOY-rah* you learned," my grandfather used to say. He had the wildest Yiddish accent. When the new year arrived, everyone said, "*Shanah tovah*"; my grandfather said, "*Sheyna Toyva*."

No one speaks like that anymore. Why? Well, modern Hebrew was designed to unify the Ashkenazi Jews and the Sephardic Jews, who spoke Ladino or Arabic, but also to get my people—the wet and phlegmy ones—to sound dry and clean. In the 1880s, a small group of Ashkenazis decided to start speaking Hebrew—and only Hebrew—with each other. Biblical Hebrew is a simple language with a limited vocabulary that, before the rise of Zionism, hadn't been a mother tongue since the second century CE. But that didn't stop Eliezer Ben-Yehuda, one of the Zionists, who forbid his son from hearing or speaking any other language, turning him into the first native speaker of modern Hebrew—and making my own childhood traumas seem entirely manageable.

Eventually, Hebrew was rethought, reconfigured, and adopted as the language of Israel, which had become a nation, if only on paper. Israeli Jews were expected to speak Hebrew, which meant they were expected to strip away the connections they'd formed with other cultures before migrating. To Ben-Yehuda—and to all nationalists of the era—language and nation were inseparable; each required the other. "The Hebrew language can live only if we revive the nation and return it to the fatherland," he wrote.

When I grew up, I spoke Yiddish, which was frowned on, even though, in my humble opinion, the language is far superior to Hebrew. Actually, I grew up speaking Yinglish, which is partly Yiddish and partly English. But all Yiddish is partly one language and partly another. American Yiddish is, basically, sixteenth-century German written with Hebrew characters, combined with Polish, Russian, Spanish, and English. Merging languages and cultures is one of our specialties, apparently, because Sephardic Jews also came up with a pidgin: Ladino, which is archaic Castilian Spanish mixed with Hebrew, along with Aramaic, Arabic, Turkish, Greek, French, and so on.

After the inquisition, Spanish Jews were expelled from the kingdom and brought Ladino to the Balkans, North Africa, the Mediterranean, Israel, and beyond. If you've seen Mel Brooks's *The History of the World*, you know what the Spanish Inquisition is:

> The Inquisition
> *What a show!*
> The Inquisition
> *Here we go!*
> We know you're wishing that we'd go away
> But the Inquisition's here, and it's here to stay!
>
> *Hey, Torquemada, whaddaya say?*
> I just got back from the auto-da-fé
> *Auto-da-fé, what's an auto-da-fé?*
> It's what you oughtn't to do but you do anyway

Anyway! Like Yiddish, Ladino moved around and morphed because of the diaspora—because of the never-ending cycle of migration, disaster, migration, assimilation, migration, oppression, etc.

Any chance that someone in the audience speaks Ladino? Spaniolish? Sephardi? Judesmo?

I didn't think so. Like Yiddish, Ladino is in decline. Hebrew, on the other hand, is flourishing, thanks to Israel. From the beginning, Zionists have treated Yiddish as a threat to Hebrew, a symbol of the diaspora. And who needs the diaspora when you've got a nation-state?

Not the Army for the Defense of the Hebrew Language, certainly. In 1930, the group attacked a Tel Aviv theater that was playing a Yiddish movie, starting a riot. Not the first prime minister of Israel, David Ben-Gurion, who called Yiddish a "foreign and ear-straining language." And not today's ethnonationalists, who're up in arms about a Yiddish production of *Fiddler on the Roof*. At the same time, there are wildly popular Israeli TV shows with Orthodox characters speaking Yiddish and singing klezmer, so who knows?

Personally, I don't have much interest in speaking Hebrew. I have even less interest in becoming Israeli. I like the diaspora. I'm fine in the diaspora. I'm not going anywhere, in part because I don't have anywhere to go. I don't have claims to land; I don't own property. I'm an eternal renter, and if I can no longer make rent—if I have to return to my homeland—then I'm headed to Queens. And I don't want to go back to Queens.

That said: "a Jew was I born." So go the lyrics of the old Yiddish tune I played when I took the stage, "*A yid bin ich geboren*." The grammar of Yiddish comes, first, from German, and then from all the other languages, cultures, and countries through which Jews have traveled. I like to think of myself in the same way: born as one thing but always becoming another, always traveling.

Did I mention that I don't want to go back to Queens?

This is what you get when you choose to spend Saturday night with the learned rabbi Benyamin Zev. I can't blame you, of course! But I can't tell you that you made the right decision. That said, you're here—which means you probably know that Israel wasn't founded because of the Holocaust, but because of a power vacuum following the collapse of the British empire. The United States moved to take the place of Britain and supported the state of Israel. And now we have this predicament: some of us think we have a claim to the land, and some of us think the land is under illegal occupation.

Guess what? I have opinions about this. Unfortunately, I'm just another Brooklyn Jew who went to Israel-Palestine in the 1990s, before the second intifada, because I thought I could solve the problem. I was invited to a peace conference and, of course, I immediately met people whose knowledge was much more extensive, and whose positions were much more radical, than my own. The conference was also devoted to feminism, as the majority of the Palestinian and Israeli activists were women. I got to meet Hanan Ashrawi, which was an honor.

Do you all know Ashrawi? One of the major forces in the PLO?

Come on! She was an ambassador for Palestinians during the first intifada, then a negotiator in the peace talks that led to the Oslo Accords, then a member of the Palestine government. But now I'm boasting. Last night, I was bragging about seeing the Ramones at CBGB; tonight, I'm going on and on about attending a peace conference, crossing the border to the West Bank, and hanging with Hanan.

When I went to Israel, the radical peace proposal being pushed was for a single-state solution: two nations sharing the same land, with Jerusalem as an international city, like the Vatican, administered by the United Nations. Two nations administered by one government, everyone a citizen: Israelis, Palestinians, and Arabs as citizens of one truly democratic country, represented by one parliament.

Somehow, a consensus formed around the two-state solution, then, recently, broke down. Now, the radical right is trying to make the status quo permanent by establishing a single state for the Jews. They want to turn the socialist state that was founded in 1948 into an ethnonationalist state. In order to protect the power of Jews, who are on the way to becoming a minority, they want to do away with democracy through violence and land grabs. And they're gaining ground.

I think it's troubling and indicative that, if you're Israeli and Jewish, your passport says so. When else in modern history has that been true? Only in Nazi Germany.

Many Jews—and many Israelis—oppose the ethnonationalist movement. Maybe some of you are in the audience?

I don't know why I'm getting into this, honestly. I didn't mean to. *Bad rabbi!* I could have kept on going with my shtick. You know, it's really easy to do Jewish comedy: all you have to do is show up and ... be Jewish. You're the joke!

I guess I feel compelled to make the point that Judaism is not Zionism. Zionism is not Judaism. I feel compelled to make the point because the equation of Judaism and Zionism has driven so many American Jews away from the religion. So many people in my generation, because of our politics, have been alienated from Jewish life. Years ago, I decided to return to temple because I realized that we'd absented ourselves from a conversation that we needed to be part of.

That wasn't the only reason I returned to temple—and recovered my lifelong dream of becoming a rabbi, if only for a night. Zionism has been subsuming American Jewish identity, but that identity was limiting when I was growing up, too. To my family, being a Jew was all about the history of the Holocaust and immigration—those were the two coordinates. I don't reject the history of the Holocaust or the experience of immigration, of course. But there's a lot more to being Jewish. There's a lot more to being human. There's a lot more to being in therapy.

For instance, you can be a Jew and be a *feygele*—a "little bird," a homosexual—as I was. You can be bookish and averse to sports, as I was. You can be a diehard fan of klezmer and punk, Barbra Streisand and no wave, as I was. You can be an Ashkenazi Jew and nearly anything else, as I was.

In other words, you can be content—you can be yourself—in the diaspora. That's what Stuart Hall, the great Jamaican-British cultural theorist, teaches us. In "Cultural Identity and Diaspora," he argues for the metaphorical meaning of diaspora, as opposed to the idea of "scattered tribes whose identity can only be secured in relation to some sacred homeland to which they must at all costs return, even if it means pushing other people into the sea." Hall explains the oppression of the Palestinians as a result of the West signing on to an antiquated and overly literal notion of diaspora. In contrast, he understands the experience of diaspora as being about "heterogeneity and diversity," not "essence or purity." He proposes "a conception of 'identity' which lives with and through, not despite, difference; by *hybridity*. Diaspora identities are those which are constantly producing and reproducing themselves anew, through transformation and difference."

I take that to heart. I learned to understand myself as queer by understanding myself as Jewish. And I learned to understand myself as Jewish by understanding myself as part of a diaspora—as having an identity that's always shifting, always in formation, and always in relation to others.

I was brought into the covenant on my eighth day on Earth. Eventually, though, I realized that the bond—which obligated Abraham to follow G-d and abandon his home, with the promise that he'd become the father of a "great nation" in the land of Canaan—is open to interpretation and negotiation from the moment the foreskin is removed.

Maybe that's TMI? I don't know. I'll tell you the formula—the compositional logic—for my work: TMI in a blender.

Who'd like a respite from the rabbi's learned disquisitions? Anyone?

How about I play some music? Not Lou Reed, sorry—you chose to come to the Shabbos performance! I'll play something different, but just as good, and just as queer. I'll play something that moves you—something that moves you to daven, at least. But pogo if you want to!

Music is central to religious observance and to queer culture. That's no mystery. But I didn't fully appreciate the connection until, in my twenties, I came across the Yiddish revival in the East Village. I was introduced to all these downtown artists and musicians who were discovering Yiddish culture, taking language classes, and experimenting with klezmer and Jewish folk music. None of this was new to me, but the effort to remake tradition—to merge the culture of my childhood with the culture where I'd found refuge—spoke to me. I revisited *nigun*, the Hasidic genre of wordless prayer, thanks to the Klezmatics, the band that reinvented Eastern European Jewish music.

In this Hebraic song, the vocalists don't sing; they chant syllables, which is meant to usher them into a sacred space. We're in the diaspora—and we have Spotify—so we can enter into a sacred space wherever and whenever we want.

[*Plays "Nign," by the Klezmatics.*]

You know Barbra Streisand, right? Of course you do! But you probably know her as the caricature: the self-assured diva with a ridiculously Jewish schnoz and a voice like *buttah*. Do you know her as a Jewish goddess with the voice of an angel and a beautiful nose that she's *never* changed? Do you know her as a queer icon? I don't think I can explain why and how Streisand became both a Jewish and gay icon without getting into trouble. I will say that her appeal to queers goes beyond Jewish culture, but her campiness is heavily inflected with Jewish humor. And I'll note that her portrait graces the cover of *Queer Theory and the Jewish Question*.

[*Holds up the book and shows the audience the cover, a portrait of Streisand by Deborah Kass.*]

Do you know Streisand as the star of *Funny Girl*, *My Name Is Barbra*, and *Color Me Barbra*? Have you seen those shows? They're amazing! She broadcast live from a department store in the first one, *My Name Is Barbra*, the black-and-white TV special she made when she was twenty-two. *Color Me Barbra*, which aired the next year, is in color and was filmed at the Philadelphia Museum of Art: Streisand flits from Renoir to Modigliani, poses as Nefertiti, sings to a caged tiger. As she sings, she stares at the camera, locks eyes with the audience, as if to say, "I'm here. I'm me."

Why do I love Barbra? Why do *we* love Barbra? Well, she's a Brooklyn Jew who could never be mistaken for anything but a Brooklyn Jew. She couldn't pass. Or, she wouldn't pass; she was always being told to get a nose job if she wanted to succeed in Hollywood, but she refused to cut off her nose to spite her race. She insisted on being in control of her performances, her image, her recordings, her career. She played to type, of course; she used her accent to comedic effect. But she didn't pander, she didn't satisfy anyone else's expectations for her. She was always herself, even though she was often playing a role, telling the story of a character—not unlike Lou Reed, not unlike a rabbi. And the meaning of her songs is inseparable from the event of the performance: her embodiment of the character, her exuberance, her emotion, her will.

How could I not love Barbra?

My mother loved Barbra. Not only did she love Barbra, she went to the same high school as Barbra, Erasmus High. Barbra was three years ahead of her. My mother didn't know Barbra, but that didn't stop my grandmother, Gloria, from telling increasingly fantastical stories about her. At first, she'd say, "Oh, such a lovely voice! Such a pretty girl! And Linda knew her from high school." Then, later, she'd say, "Oh, such a nice girl! We had her over for Passover.

She sang. She sang for us! Can you imagine?" I'd bring friends home when I was in my twenties and she'd tell these stories about Barbra eating her *haroseth*. They'd believe her! My mother and I would stand behind her, wagging our fingers, mouthing, "No, no, no."

Eventually, my grandmother insisted that every famous—and not-so-famous—Brooklyn Jew had gone through my mother's high school. And half of them had eaten matzo with us.

Here's the truth: I do not have a personal relationship with Barbra Streisand. I've never met her. I *feel* like I know her, though. Because I've davened with her—or to her. She's brought me and many others to prayer.

I'm going to play her rendition of Avinu Malkeinu, the prayer that marks the beginning of the new year, and asks G-d to forgive our sins and grant us blessings. Streisand recorded the song—complete with orchestra and chorus—singing the first verse in English and the rest in Hebrew.

> Hear our prayer
> We have sinned before Thee
> Have compassion upon us and upon our children
> Help us bring an end to pestilence, war, and famine
> Cause all hate and oppression to vanish from the earth
> Inscribe us for blessing in the Book of Life
> Let the new year be a good year for us

Avinu malkeinu sh'ma kolenu
Avinu malkeinu chatanu l'faneycha
Avinu malkeinu alkenu chamol aleynu
V'al olaleynu v'tapenu

If you're davening at temple, if you're asking for compassion, you're forgiven any vows you've made to G-d. If you've made a promise to a friend and you haven't delivered, you're on your own; it's between the two of you. That's what I like about Judaism: you're on your own.

You can't expect G-d to intervene, but you can curse at G-d. How many of you know this?

When my mother died, I went to Rabbi Lippmann, who taught me about the tradition of angry prayer. She said, "You can curse at G-d—it's OK!" She told me that you can yell at G-d! G-d can take it. And that helped me. I needed a divinity to abuse. I felt like a prophet—prophets are always angry at G-d.

When I was raging at G-d, I thought: whatever I say and do is between me and my maker. That doesn't mean G-d was going to do anything for me. The forgiveness of vows doesn't depend on G-d acting in the world, punishing people who eat ham sandwiches and fulfilling the wishes of those who abstain. I knew that I'd be offered nothing but forgiveness. But that's all I needed: to scream and curse and sin and be forgiven. I couldn't do that with Rabbi Lippmann—not that I'd ever curse at her.

Back to Barbra: "Do it for Your sake and deliver us. ... Do it for the sake of Your great mercy." Forgive us.

The forgiving of vows was especially important to Jews—and became central to the observance of the high holidays—during the Spanish Inquisition, when many Jews were forced to convert under pain of death. When we say *kol nidrei*—"all vows"—at the beginning of the Yom Kippur service, we're repeating the legal formula that enabled converts to return to Judaism. Kol nidrei goes in and out of fashion: after the Haskalah—the nineteenth-century Jewish Enlightenment—the rabbis wanted to do away with the forgiveness of vows. They were aggravated by anti-Semites using kol nidrei to denounce Jews as untrustworthy, even though Jews are only let off the hook for promises made to G-d. And, anyway, they thought vows were too binding, too risky, even for rabbis. Vows create expectations, after all, and expectations set you up for failure. That's been my experience, at least.

Here's one of the holier versions of the prayer, recorded by the Electric Prunes, who took some liberties with the words.

> All the vows
> And guarantees

All the noble promises to God
We left unaccomplished

From the last day of atonement
To this day of atonement
Now come to us in peace
These we regret, we regret

May God help us to endure
The hardships of life
With fortitude
And sufferance
Amen

Judaism changes all the time. One day, the Jews are being killed if they don't convert; the next, the Electric Prunes are doing "Kol Nidrei" with fuzzed-out electric guitars and Barbra Streisand is going platinum with an album that features "Avinu Malkeinu." That's fascinating, right? Streisand forced Jewish ethnicity into popular culture, into the entertainment industry; she made a claim on her identity. The more I do these shows, the more I wonder how to do what Streisand did. I'm dealing with that question right now, in real time—and I'm no Barbra Streisand. I've met her, though! My mom actually went to high school with her. They were friendly—very close—*extremely* close. Such a beautiful, kind girl. And her voice! *Like an angel.*

I'm sorry. Am I performing my ethnicity for your entertainment? Yeah, I suppose. I won't do religious rituals, though, not for ten dollars per ticket. But perform my ethnicity? Sure. Isn't that standard fare? *Seinfeld*, *Everybody Loves Raymond*, *Cake Boss*—I'm a little dated with my television references. What's a contemporary example?

[*Audience member shouts:* "The Sopranos!" *Laughter follows.*]

Yes—proof enough that we're used to people performing their ethnicities for the sake of entertainment. There's a durable market. And, at the same time, we know that the performance can serve purposes other than—higher than—entertainment, right? We know the difference between trying to get laughs by playing to type and trying to get recognition by making a claim to an identity.

In other words, I suspect that entertainment was not Streisand's only motivation. I'll have to ask her when I see her at Passover.

Barbra Streisand isn't a rabbi, but she plays one in the movies. Or, at least, she plays a would-be rabbi in *Yentl*, her adaptation of the Isaac Bashevis Singer story: she's the daughter of a rabbi in an Eastern European shtetl in 1904, and she's intent on studying Torah. But Yentl is a woman. "They're talking about life, the mysteries of the universe," she says, "and I'm learning how to tell a herring from a carp!" So she runs away from home and pretends to be a man in order to enter a yeshiva. At the end, she runs away again—to America. To the diaspora!

I like to imagine Yentl ending up in New York City and hanging out with Abraham Joshua Heschel, the great scholar who, to me, epitomizes the twentieth-century rabbi. Born in Poland, he escaped the Nazis, but much of his family was killed in the Holocaust. He was able to flee to New York thanks to Jews in academia, and he spent the rest of his life on the Upper West Side, writing book after book after book. Heschel was similar to the Frankfurt School philosophers in his response to the war: he was skeptical of rationalism, scientism, and bureaucracy, which he saw as enabling the destruction. But he was mostly concerned with spirituality—or with the erosion of spirituality, especially among Jews. In reckoning with the Holocaust, he questioned the Haskalah, which had pushed Jews to embrace modernization, secularism, and nationalism. He saw the Haskalah as a "great challenge to Jews around the world."

I don't know if I feel challenged by the Haskalah; I don't feel threatened. I see that moment as an important development in Jewish history and thought, one that emerges from Jews around the world engaging with all kinds of philosophy and theology for centuries and centuries. That said, I'm sympathetic to the idea that the Haskalah led to religious identity being subsumed by national identity, and mysticism being traded for nationalism. And I'm really taken with the notion of spirituality that Heschel proposes in response: "radical amazement." In *Man Is Not Alone*, he argues that to be spiritual is to encounter the world as phenomenal, incredible; to take nothing for granted. When you do this—when you experience "radical amazement"—you're in the presence of divinity.

Of course, this notion of religion flies in the face of reason. You can't explain or systematize that experience of G-d, right? You can't turn "radical amazement" into the basis for an ethnonationalist state. And that's the point: G-d doesn't make plans for people to execute or reserve land for us to occupy. Heschel looks to the mystics—and the Kabbalah—for an alternative. He describes them as the source of the "bold and dangerously paradoxical idea that not only is G-d necessary to man but man is also necessary to G-d, to the unfolding of his plans in this world." G-d's plan is *tikkun olam*, to repair the world.

I love Heschel. How many people have read his work?

[*Surveys the audience.*]

Three people. It's not a test! I just want to know who's with me. If you all raise your hands, we'll have nothing to talk about; I'll have to ask *you* questions.

Maybe I *should* ask you questions?

[*Points to audience member.*]

Why did you read Heschel?

[*Audience member replies.*]

Because you told me to!

[*Bordowitz replies.*]

What can I say? I'm always telling people to read Heschel. His work has been incredibly useful for me as an activist. He turned a few lines of Torah and volumes of commentary in the Talmud into the basis for Jewish liberation theology. He asked great, challenging, consequential questions. The most famous one: how do we believe in G-d after the Holocaust? This was an urgent question for my grandfather's generation, for those who couldn't understand how G-d had let the Jews be slaughtered. Heschel said, "Why are you blaming G-d for Auschwitz? People did that to people." A brilliant retort.

G-d is the reason for existence, but G-d isn't responsible for all that exists, all that happens. G-d is the immanent cause of everything, but G-d didn't form the world out of nothing. People mix up the notion of G-d as the universe—or vice versa—with pantheism. But, really, that's more of a Romantic idea. That's not the same as Baruch Spinoza, the seventeenth-century Jewish philosopher, challenging the traditional understanding of G-d as a transcendent creator. Nevertheless, people accused Spinoza of pantheism—and they still do.

How many of you have read Spinoza?

[*Several audience members raise hands.*]

Some of you. Not enough, though! Spinoza made the radical argument that everything follows from the divine nature, meaning that G-d doesn't exist without the world; the two are inextricable, interdependent. How could G-d have chosen to create or not create the world?

Spinoza belonged to an orthodox Jewish community, and he was banished for his beliefs. That's hard to do, by the way: there's no central authority in Jewish religious life, there's no Vatican. Congregations decide how to deal with people with contrary opinions, and hardly anyone gets kicked out. I don't really know why Spinoza's fellow Jews got so angry at him. He does, at least, subscribe to prime causality: everything is attributed to G-d, as opposed to causality coming from everywhere, or every phenomenon being dependent on every other, which is a Buddhist principle.

That's a lecture for another time: the Buddhist monk—the obvious follow-up to the rock star, rabbi, and comedian.

Perhaps Spinoza got into trouble because he suggested that G-d doesn't act; G-d doesn't have a human consciousness. Which means that G-d isn't watching people, punishing them for sinning, worrying about them eating ham sandwiches. G-d doesn't arbitrate morality or impose order on society. In Spinoza's view, the consequences of actions aren't so much about morality as the fabric of existence—physical laws, even. Spinoza's world is rational, mathematical. He compares G-d to a triangle: all existence flows from the divine nature, just as three angles of a triangle add up to 180 degrees.

I believe in G-d—all 180 degrees. But I've wrestled with the question of belief all my life. A few years ago, I decided that I don't need to know what G-d is or does in order to believe. In fact, I need to believe in something that exceeds reason, something that can't be defined. Where does that leave me? Well, I'm into negative theology: I'm interested in what G-d is *not*. For instance, G-d is not like a human; the divine body is not like my body.

If G-d's body *were* like mine, I might have to rethink my belief, and I don't imagine I'd be the only one.

[*Looks down, evaluates his body, shrugs.*]

Too bad for G-d, though, because I know where to get a pretty flattering suit for cheap.

In much of Jewish lore and thought, G-d doesn't have a body at all. G-d has masculine and feminine principles and names: the Shechinah is the female manifestation of divinity, as I mentioned, and *Hashem* has no gender. Nevertheless, people are said to be *made in the image* of G-d. What does that mean? For a long time, many rabbis interpreted the Bible literally, and asserted that G-d looks like us. Other rabbis, however, suggested that, while humanity is made in the likeness of G-d's image, that doesn't mean G-d has a knowable physical form.

The Talmud is full of debates about how—or if—to represent divinity, and about the relationship between the image and the idea. My sense of G-d isn't anthropomorphic or anthropocentric. And that extends from envisioning G-d to comprehending G-d's role: I don't believe that G-d has a human conscience or intervenes in our affairs. G-d doesn't *care*, I like to say. Not because G-d is insensitive, but because G-d isn't human. G-d is a habit or pattern.

G-d is the ineffable. G-d is what you can't describe. G-d exceeds representation.

What does G-d *do*, you ask? Well, G-d isn't the subject of a verb; G-d isn't a person who performs actions that we can see and describe. Honestly, I have no idea what G-d *does*—but I'm sure it's very important.

Recently, I was talking about my view of G-d with a close friend who's terminally ill. He's not religious, and he knows that I am. He asked me, "How have we known each other for thirty years and I've never asked why you believe in G-d?" So we finally had the conversation. I told him that G-d needs us more than we need G-d.

My friend, Douglas, was gay and grew up in the 1950s in Idaho. He saw how abusive and damaging religion could be; he saw how people were thrown out of their communities for being different. He became a Marxist, a gay liberationist, and an art historian—a brilliant intellectual—so he had a very clear sense of why people might not embrace religion. And I understood. I've had many friends who've said, "If we could just get rid of religion, we'd be done with oppression, war, etc." I disagree, of course. Wars tend to be fought due to scarcity, and that's what we have to eliminate: obscenely unequal access to resources. On that, at least, Douglas and I could agree.

Douglas never had a come-to-Jesus moment, but he did read the Bible—I bought him a very academic edition, with maps of the ancient world—and he got into Buddhist meditation. I talked to him about how, to me, G-d is like a habit or pattern, and I talked to him about the value of having faith in something I can't define. While I was caring for Douglas, I recognized that returning to religion had a lot to do with loss. Before Douglas got sick, my mother, grandfather, and grandmother had died. I was disoriented; I was going to see Douglas during the day and night, and I had the sense of time being distorted. I needed stability, routine, and sustenance, so I turned to G-d.

I'm not ashamed to admit that: I have a weak constitution, I guess!

I've had versions of the conversation I had with Douglas many times, with many people. I came of age as an AIDS activist, and caring for Douglas brought me back to the years when I spent much of my time with friends who were sick or dying. I was very, very ill, too, before the invention of protease inhibitors in 1996. I didn't expect to be here; I didn't expect to live to be thirty-five, forty, or fifty. I'm alive because of luck, not because of G-d. I don't believe that G-d saved me and let dozens of my friends—hundreds of thousands of people—die. Do you?

Do you believe that G-d brought us protease inhibitors? Do you believe that G-d changed how Americans perceive those who are infected with HIV? Do you believe that G-d pushed politicians and public-health officials to address the crisis? I hope not. Because *we* did that. *We* demanded funding for research. *We* demanded to be recognized as human beings. *We* demanded government action.

What does this have to do with the history of the Jews? In the Torah, there's a midrash about the Hebrews fleeing the pharaoh's soldiers during the exodus from Egypt. After freeing the Hebrews, the pharaoh had changed his mind, and by the time the Hebrews arrive at the Red Sea, the Egyptian soldiers are on their heels. They're left with no path; they need a miracle. You've seen the movie: the Hebrews are facing the sea and G-d says, "I'll perform a miracle. I'll part the sea. First, though, one person has to enter the water. And not Moses." (He knows he's got Moses.)

Moses looks around. He's like, "Hey, let's have an act of faith, OK?!?" And someone—perhaps Nahshon, a prince of the tribe of Judah—jumps into the water. The sea parts.

The whole scene is described in a few lines of Torah. From those lines, Jewish liberation theologists have deduced that divine intervention requires human action. According to Heschel, the Hebrews discovered that "the G-d of nature is the G-d of history, and the way to know Him is to do his will."

In other words, G-d's will isn't expressed through a hand reaching out from the sky to prevent you from eating a ham sandwich—or to stop one group of people from massacring another group of people. We can't expect G-d to tell us what to do, then make sure we don't mess up. We have to understand the relationship between the three paths to G-d: worship, learning, and action. Heschel suggested that, instead of treating G-d like a genie or a judge, we consider what we *really* want from G-d. What did Heschel want? Wonder. "Never once in my life did I ask G-d for success or wisdom or power or fame," he wrote. "I asked for wonder, and G-d gave it to me."

Rather than ask G-d for a million dollars, or a Maserati—or victory in armed conflict, or the exclusive right to a swathe of land—let's consider how much G-d needs us. G-d needs us more than we need G-d. Why else would G-d create humans? What purpose do we serve?

In *God in Search of Man*, Heschel challenges Maimonides's idea of G-d as existing apart from humans, as transcendent. He says that the divine and the human are entwined, and he insists on "divine pathos": G-d needs people. G-d is enfeebled without people. G-d's kingdom on Earth can't be realized without humans fulfilling the Commandments. G-d's power comes from the work that we do in the name of G-d. And G-d's existence depends on human witnesses. Giving voice to G-d, Heschel writes: "When you are my witnesses, then I am God, but when you are not my witnesses, then I am, as it were, not God."

Can I get a witness?

If I could call Nechama Leibowitz, I'd ask her to be my witness. What would you ask her?

I'd ask her about Exodus, which I was reading today for *Parashah Bo*. Do you know about *Parashah Bo*? Are you in my reading group?

[*Silence and tentative head-shaking in the audience.*]

Well, I wouldn't be surprised if you were: the reading group is worldwide and open to all. Every Saturday, thousands of Jews read and discuss the same portion of the Torah. I wake up, open the *Chabad* website, check the section of the Torah, and see what Rashi has to say. Today's Exodus, so I've been going back to Liebowitz, who said that G-d brought the Israelites out of slavery, but then brought them into spiritual bondage. G-d wasn't doing a good deed, he wasn't going around and freeing oppressed people. He cut a deal: I'll get you out of Egypt, but you have to live by my laws, you have to abide by the covenant.

What if the Jews hadn't agreed? What if they hadn't obeyed? Where would G-d be? There's a Hasidic story about children playing hide and seek: one kid finds a great hiding spot and the others abandon the game. The kid who's hiding sits still for hours. "I am *so* good at this game," he thinks. Eventually, though, he realizes that no one is looking for him. He leaves his hiding spot and, realizing that his playmates have left, he cries. He's distressed to learn that no one has been searching for him. The boy, of course, is G-d. G-d needs us to search and search, even while recognizing that divinity is everywhere and, thus, impossible to find.

Leibowitz, writing after the Holocaust, was eager to differentiate between submitting to G-d and submitting to "superior orders." The latter isn't a matter of faith, but an excuse to avoid moral responsibility, to avoid questioning power. She talks about this in a commentary on Exodus, which explains how the Jews rebelled and were liberated—or how they liberated themselves.

Stop me if you've heard this one before: the Jews were in Egypt, and the pharaoh ordered two midwives, Shiphrah and Puah, to kill every newborn Jew. But, fearing G-d, they disobeyed the pharaoh.

Again: a few lines of Torah, volumes and volumes of commentary. In the Torah, it's unclear if Shiphrah and Puah are the only midwives that deliver Hebrew children or if they stand in for all the midwives; it's unclear if they're Hebrew or if they work with Hebrew families. But they're credited with stopping the ethnic cleansing, and, in midrashim, they become heroic and enormously symbolic figures.

Scholars have speculated that Shiphrah and Puah inspired a revolt among the midwives, or even organized the midwives, orchestrating a rebellion. They've debated whether Shiphrah and Puah were Hebrew or Egyptian names. If they were Hebrew, that points to the possibility of resistance among the Jews, despite the conditions and consequences. If they were Egyptian, that points to the possibility of Jews finding allies among the oppressed wherever they live, wherever they travel.

Leibowitz uses the story to make a remarkable point about the bonds of morality being stronger than those of nationality or ethnicity. "If we accept that the midwives were Egyptian," she writes, "a very vital message becomes apparent." Following orders—submitting to the will of the authorities, who claim to be enacting G-d's plans—is antithetical to Judaism. Exodus "contrasts the brutal decrees of enslavement and massacre initiated by

Pharaoh and supported by government and people with the G-d fearing 'civil disobedience' of the midwives," Leibowitz writes, countering the standard interpretation. "Neither moral courage nor sheer wickedness are ethnically or nationally determined qualities. Moab and Ammon produced a Ruth and Naamah respectively; Egypt two righteous midwives."

Technically, the Hebrews in Israel weren't enslaved, which is why Exodus refers to "servitude" and "bondage." The previous pharaoh had invited them to dwell in Egypt, and allowed them to do whatever Canaanites did: pray to whichever god they wanted, perform whichever ritual sacrifices they wanted. But the Jews flourished and multiplied, and the pharaoh got worried: What if Egypt is attacked and the Jews join forces with the enemy? What if they realize that they don't have to tolerate being oppressed, and they rise up? So the pharaoh taxes them, forces them to work, subjects them to violence, and orders their sons to be killed. Then, finally, after Moses demands the freedom of his people, after the plagues, after the angel of death, and so on, the pharaoh banishes the Hebrews.

The Book of Exodus is the first time in the Torah that the Hebrews are referred to as a people—the first time that the name of Israel is invoked. Before G-d addresses the Canaanites as the people of Israel, the pharaoh calls them Israelites, distinguishing them from those who come from and belong in Egypt. Exodus marks the origin of the idea of Israel as a nation, and of the Hebrews as defined by the nation they've been promised—or the nation they've been charged with inventing on the land they've been promised. The book is the beginning of the story of emancipation being contingent on the Jews having a nation—and being confused for the possession of a nation.

How else can we understand Exodus? What questions can we ask of this story?

We can ask how Exodus has been used to identify Jews as Israelis, and Israelis as Jews. And we can challenge that Zionist interpretation, which minimizes so many of the wonderful and terrible things that define and differentiate us—and provide us with fodder for therapy. Zionism pushes the wet and phlegmy among us to sound dry and clean, to say *toe-ruh* instead of *TOY-rah*. It naturalizes the obscenely literal understanding of diaspora: the promise of a Jewish homeland—the covenant with G-d—as requiring that Jews install themselves in Canaan, and get rid of whomever else happens to be there. Why? Because that's G-d's plan, and we are but his humble, nuclear-armed servants.

To me, though, Exodus gives us the basis to reject what Stuart Hall calls the "old, imperializing, hegemonizing ... form of 'ethnicity.'" Exodus gives us the courage to say, "Tomorrow is *TOY-rah*." Exodus gives us the reason to understand ourselves as a people in diaspora, with freedom as an everlasting horizon and not a nation-state, not a passport stamped with "Jew."

Recently, as I've been reading Exodus, I've been thinking about the history of the United States: the shift from the enslavement of Africans to the mass incarceration and state-sanctioned murder of Black people. I've been thinking about the oppression and emancipation of the Hebrews in relation to the assimilation of Jews in my lifetime—the transition from "ethnic" to white, from being different to being ... similar enough. And I've been thinking about liberation as a promise that is never fulfilled, a process that is never completed, rather than something we get as part of a transaction with a deity or government.

In Exodus, Moses goes up to the mountain to get the law, and he doesn't come back for a really long time. The Israelis get antsy: they don't know what's going on; they don't know what they're doing or where they're going; they don't know who they are. Are we in the promised land? Are we free? Are we the chosen people? They have a crisis of faith. They worship the golden calf and dress in "costly array," according to Cecil B. DeMille's *Ten Commandments*, at least.

Ultimately, they wander for years and years, without finding answers. The generation of Hebrews that was liberated from Egypt never really lived, they spent their lives wandering. Why? So that the next generation would understand the meaning of freedom via wandering and not by securing a nation-state.

What else does Exodus teach us? Ancient Egypt is everywhere. And the promised land is always around the next bend. But we keep wandering, right? We keep marching through the wilderness. Why? To get closer and closer; to close the gap between the promise and reality. For that to happen, we have to march with others. We have to "make the world worthy of redemption," as Heschel writes.

Redemption isn't a debt that's owed to us or a contract that we can execute. We're not going to be redeemed by running down the clock or building separation walls; the messianic era isn't going to arrive thanks to our patience or national security measures.

The Torah doesn't tell us what to do in order to bring about redemption. The Torah doesn't tell us how to act—or, at least, the Torah doesn't provide a comprehensive framework that enables us to judge everything we say and do as good or bad, as expediting or delaying the arrival of the messiah. I'm fascinated with the Torah—I read the Torah—because I believe in the fundamental principle that the book yields infinite interpretations. The Torah pushes me to confront ideas that I don't agree with, too; I may not like those ideas, but I have to figure out how to understand and assimilate them. The Torah is like life, in that respect.

Rabbi Lippmann taught me not to look to the Torah for instruction on what to do, for morals. The Torah isn't a book of morals; it's about people trying to be good and coming up short. The Torah is about failure. What happens when you fail? You keep trying; you keep asking questions, you keep interpreting. You don't go to hell, at least.

Remember: for Jews, there's no heaven or hell.

[*Addresses someone in the front row whose head is vigorously shaking.*]

You disagree?

[*Audience member replies.*]

Well, I think it's funny that you're stating this categorically. I've heard in other versions of Jewish theology that hell does exist.

[*Bordowitz replies.*]

Well, it's up for debate, like everything in Judaism. We've had to deal with Aristotle, Spinoza, and however many other philosophical ruptures, which have caused us to reconsider scriptures, beliefs, and the nature of divinity. Since Judaism exists in the diaspora, we've had to contend with philosophies from around the world, which has led to variants of Jewish thought. The Queens variant circa 1977 indicates that Judaism is *soft* on hell. There are Jewish folk tales with malevolent figures that resemble the devil, or the dark side of G-d: ghosts, demons, werewolves. Pick up Joachim Neugroschel's *The Shtetl*, an excellent anthology of translations of Yiddish folklore, or *Great Tales of Jewish Fantasy and the Occult*, and you'll find accounts of heaven and hell—or versions of reality that feel like heaven or hell.

Hell is not an enormous cave where the sinners burn for all of eternity. Hell is not defined as a place. Heaven exists, though, at least in Jewish liberation theology: heaven exists on Earth—right now! But you have to be able to see heaven. You have to be able to reach out and hold heaven. And to do so you have to work for liberation; you have to repair the world. There's a similar idea of heaven on Earth in Christian liberation theology, and in many other religions: Hinduism, Buddhism, Islam.

[*Audience member speaks.*]

What about the afterlife?

[*Bordowitz replies.*]

I'll respond with a joke. There's this guy—let's call him Morty. Morty dies and appears before G-d, who says, "Welcome, Morty! I'm going to take you through the stages of the afterlife. In the end, we'll arrive at the one where you belong." G-d opens a door. He and Morty walk into a ballroom where a twenty-piece orchestra is playing. There are countless people talking, eating, singing, dancing—they're even dancing on the tables, they're enjoying themselves so much. They're having a wild time. And there's a huge, unbeatable spread—a buffet! Morty's favorite.

Morty says, "Amazing! And this is only the first door?!?"

G-d says, "Yeah, wait, wait, there's more!"

They go through another door, into another party. It's really classy. Not as many people, but ... hors d'oeuvres, a nice combo, several couples doing the cha-cha. Morty says, "Very nice. I can definitely see the virtue in this."

They go through the third door, into an empty room. G-d says, "You've arrived! This is heaven."

There's no one else in the room. It's totally quiet. Crickets.

Morty looks really disappointed. He says, "This, well—this is ... this is it?"

G-d replies, "What? For one person I should hire a band?"

Why is that so funny? Only one person made it to heaven, right? That's funny. And, of course, Jews don't even believe in heaven. But the essence of the joke is the question: how did you live your life? If you're honest with yourself, you know that you're not always fair and kind to others. You're human; you fail, you fall short. You're no Morty. He's infallible, which is why he's the only one in heaven.

As for hell, the version that I know—besides the one in which I'm living right now—is that you don't wake up when the messiah comes. That's it! You're not woken up. You wait forever.

You know that plenty of Jews are waiting for the messiah, right? The basic scenario is the same as the one in all the TV shows about the living dead (which may or may not have been written by Jews): the messiah's going to resurrect those who are deserving, however they've decayed. According to Orthodox Jews, if you lead a good life, you'll be reanimated, cleaned up, given a fresh suit, and then you'll enjoy heaven on earth for all eternity. You'll experience the world as right and righteous. As I speak, Jewish kids in Crown Heights are laying out fresh clothes before they go to bed, in case the messiah comes in the middle of the night. It's true!

Walter Benjamin picked up on this feeling of constant expectation when he said that every moment is "the narrow gate through which the messiah might enter." After the rise of Hitler—and right before taking his own life while attempting to flee the Nazis—Benjamin was grappling with the relationship between history and revolution. He came up with the idea of "messianic time," importing what he'd learned from Gershom Scholem about the Kabbalah into Western philosophy. He thought about the messiah in relation to a sense of hope, a sense of continuity between past, present, and future. But he wasn't saying that we have to be sure our clothes are ready. He was saying that the failures of the past are redeemed by the present; the dead are redeemed by the living. He was saying that we have to act as if anything can happen at any moment.

Redemption is about our faith *and* actions—that's what constitutes G-d, remember? G-d needs us more than we need G-d.

Here's Heschel again: "The meaning of redemption is to reveal the holy that is concealed, to disclose the divine that is suppressed. Every person is called upon to be a redeemer, and redemption takes place every moment, every day." In other words, divine intervention requires human action. That's why Heschel marched with Martin Luther King in Selma: both of them believed that human deeds have an impact on G-d—they called G-d "the most moved Mover." Marching together was a way of worshiping together, moving G-d together. When Heschel came back from Selma, he was asked if he had found time to pray, and he said, "I felt my legs were praying." He might have been paraphrasing Frederick Douglas, who said that he prayed to G-d for twenty years and got no answer, then he started praying with his legs and everything changed.

For a long time, that idea—the nexus between what we do and the revelation of G-d's power—has been at the core of my politics.

In the 1980s, after my friends started dying from AIDS, and after I was diagnosed, I joined ACT UP. We hit the subways, wheat-pasting the walls with graphic images that showed how to put on condoms and clean syringes, because there was no public effort to educate people about AIDS. We made public-access shows about getting diagnosed with AIDS, caring for your body, and pressuring the FDA. We produced educational videos for—and with—teenagers about coming out and practicing safe sex, then got them distributed in high schools.

Yes, a video on sex for queer high schoolers! We made the video, *It Is What It Is*, with the Hetrick-Martin Institute's LGBTQ high school, with the support of the Board of Education. Can you imagine? I went to the Board of Ed, met with officials, and went through the script line by line. We agreed that "eat me" is too sexually provocative, but "bite me"? Acceptable. The Board of Ed approved the final video, which was distributed to schools throughout the five boroughs, and even won awards. Then a high school in Queens—my old borough—objected, new members were elected to the board, and the video went from being celebrated to being at the top the list of banned AIDS education propaganda. I was heartbroken. What we'd done was so radical and so meaningful to the students: we got real queer teens to speak to each other.

I wished I'd been able to see a video like that when I was growing up. That said, by the time I finished school and moved to Manhattan, I'd gotten to be pretty sophisticated. I was queer, but I thought of myself as beyond labels. I was an anarchist whose sexuality couldn't be defined by gender. I was a lapsed Jew from Yiddish Brooklyn who was into nineteenth-century European Decadence. I was an East Village punk who got fucked up and made the no wave scene before heading to the disco. I was no West Village clone—I was against uniforms, against homogeneity, against groupthink. But after I was diagnosed—after I got involved with ACT UP—I changed. I didn't want to define myself in opposition to what were, essentially, my people. There was so much else to oppose. And so many people—gay people—to bring together in opposition. I wanted to submit to those people. I wanted to understand myself in relation to them. I wanted to work toward redemption with them.

I went back to my days at shul—to Rabbi Gordon and Exodus and Nechama Leibowitz—and wondered what I could do to make the world worthy of redemption. I started to think about my life as a queer person in America in relation to my family's experience as Jews in a foreign land, a foreign homeland. I went back to temple. And I asked myself: what am I doing when I read the Torah, when I daven, when I have a conversation about the nature of G-d? I'm engaging in the endless effort to understand the ineffable. And what does that effort imply? How, in seeking to understand the relationship between faith and action, in reckoning with the state of the world and the role of forces beyond my control or understanding, am I opening myself up to others? How am I recognizing my own vulnerability as something that I have in common with others, something that binds me to others—and as a reason to march with others?

Judith Butler writes about this in *Giving an Account of Oneself*, which connects Emmanuel Levinas—the great philosopher of ethics and Talmud scholar—and Jean Laplanche, the French psychoanalyst. Very few Levinas devotees read both the ethics and the Talmud scholarship, much less connect the two. But, amazingly, Butler clocks both. And she reconciles Levinas's ethical and religious writings with Laplanche's theory of the unconscious. She asks what to make of the feeling that I *own* my unconscious, inasmuch as that makes me who I am, even though everyone is constituted by "the address of the other," which means that everyone is "dispossessed" from day one. In order to become myself, I have to deal with the fact that I don't *belong* to myself; I have to experience dispossession as enriching, not as a loss.

Invoking Levinas, Butler suggests that "self-preservation is not the highest goal, and the defense of a narcissistic point of view not the most urgent psychic need." We're "impinged upon" from the cradle to the grave, whether we want to be or not, because we're vulnerable and beholden to others. But that'll never change. Like Barbra Streisand, you have to embrace who you are, I guess. If you don't have Barbra's voice and will, what're you going to do? You can see an analyst, you can get a prescription, or you can march with others. I'm here to recommend all three.

Butler agrees, more or less. She says that you can fend off the psychic dispossession "only by prizing the asociality of the subject over and against a difficult and intractable, even sometimes unbearable relationality." In my experience, though, relationality can be highly bearable. I feel myself relating to others when I sing in wordless prayer at temple, when I sway back and forth with my fellow congregants, when I imagine people throughout time and around the world doing the same. Prayer is all about address—addressing another. It's about giving an account of oneself to another, and being *other* to *another*. It's about serving and being served. Prayer is an ethical stance—a disposition toward humility, whether you believe in G-d or not.

What can we do with this disposition, with this humility? We can act with—in relation to—others, and we can act as if divine intervention is contingent on us doing so. We can give ourselves over to messianic time, especially in moments of crisis.

Benjamin argued that the most perilous moments of crisis aren't when everything threatens to change, but when "the status quo threatens to be preserved." To keep this from happening, we have to untether our present from our notion of the past, which tends to provide the rationale for things being the way they are. We have to treat the present not as following from the past but as holding the possibility of a "counter-rhythmic rupture."

I think about messianic time in terms of HIV/AIDS and the treatment of people with the disease—in terms of the history of the pandemic as well as our interpretation of that history, which conditions what we do in the present. Somehow, we've gotten the idea that the disease only afflicts gay white men, or that the AIDS crisis is over, even though the crisis is just beginning—even though nearly one million people died from AIDS-related illnesses last year, 60 percent of them in sub-Saharan Africa. But the world we live in tomorrow doesn't have to be anything like the one we live in today. We can change the future by changing the relationship between the present and the past. "Every moment is the gate through which the messiah might enter."

That's how I feel now, and that's how I felt in the 1980s, when my friends started dying. I remember watching *A Virus Has No Morals*, directed by Rosa von Praunheim, the famous German filmmaker and gay liberation activist. Have any of you seen *A Virus Has No Morals*?

[*One audience member raises a hand.*]

One person! You can confirm that the film was, for good reason, unpopular. It's a sci-fi thriller about an HIV-positive gang confronting a disinterested society by infecting random people until the government does something. It's a John Waters–esque satire of the AIDS crisis. At the time, I hated the film! As I said, I was postering the subway, organizing die-ins, occupying the FDA headquarters, barging into meetings at pharmaceutical companies, setting off smoke bombs at medical conferences, and so on. I was trying to change minds and policies, and show that queer people were not the threat—ignorance, homophobia, and government inaction were the threat.

You know what *A Virus Has No Morals* suggests? We *are* the threat. We are the threat to upstanding citizens who believe they're safe because—why else?—they're straight, they have money, they have status. Or, at least, we'll turn ourselves into the threat in order to get what we want; we'll use the virus as a tool, and we'll show no empathy—no mercy!—to those who stand in our way.

Now, though, I have a very different understanding of *A Virus Has No Morals*. I think of the film as a shock to the system—a shock even to viewers like me. If we're in a state of crisis, if we're going to make sure the status quo isn't preserved, we need *A Virus*

Has No Morals as much as we need die-ins, postering campaigns, and sex-ed videos. We need all of it.

We need to use the virus as a tool: a tool to get drugs into bodies, universal health care, affordable housing, prison abolition, and the end of patents for life-saving drugs. We need all of it.

We need to convince the world that anyone can be a vector of contagion. Anyone can be Benyamin Zev. Or Robert Zimmerman! Anything can happen at any moment.

When AIDS started to spread in the US, most people could easily tell themselves that the *vectors* belonged to another realm. So that's what they told themselves! GRID, right? "*Gay-related* immune deficiency."

Turns out that the epidemiological picture was inaccurate: there were articles about small groups of men getting Kaposi's sarcoma, a form of cancer, and pneumocystis pneumonia. Then the CDC's *Morbidity and Mortality Weekly Report* speculated that these diseases, which were very rare in young, healthy men, were attributable to "some aspect of a shared lifestyle." Which meant that those of us who shared the lifestyle were a threat to everyone else.

In fact, the epidemiological record showed that various opportunistic infections that would come to define HIV were cropping up all over the city. All kinds of people were getting sick. Tuberculosis was exploding in the Bronx. And thousands of people were dying in Africa. Looking back at the data, it's clear that there was a burgeoning pandemic. But the medical establishment continued to define AIDS as a disease for gay men.

The CDC didn't recognize many of these opportunistic infections—some of which afflicted people other than gay men—as indicating AIDS until 1991, after ACT UP organized a series of protests at the Atlanta headquarters. Our model was the feminist health care movement—*Our Bodies, Ourselves*—and we saw that women were being excluded by the CDC's definition of AIDS. They didn't share the "lifestyle," so they weren't diagnosed, which meant they weren't given care or assistance from the government. Eventually, the CDC redefined AIDS, but only enough to include infections that afflicted women.

How'd I feel back then? How'd I feel as we fought and got sick, as we fought and died? I can't quite say. I guess I felt like a vector of contagion. I felt like a Hasidic boy getting ready for the messiah. I felt like a character in a Lou Reed song. I felt like an angry prophet. I felt like a body out of time. I felt like I feel now.

I was pissed. I'm still pissed! What can I do, though? I'll continue to search. I'll continue to believe. I'll continue to act. I'll be pissed all my life, but, well ... that doesn't mean I don't have faith. That doesn't mean I don't have will. That doesn't mean I don't like to dance.

[*Applause.*]

Chapter 3:
The Comedian

Welcome! Welcome to the Concord. Or am I playing Kutsher's Hotel tonight? Grossinger's? What's the year? Is it 5705? I hope so—a great time for a weekend in the Borscht Belt. The best performers, the best buffets. And, from the looks of you, the best audiences in the diaspora!

I'm Benyamin Zev, and I welcome you to my fantasy: a Jewish variety show circa 5705 *and* 2018, upstate *and* downtown. It's my fantasy, so I don't have to choose where or when the show happens; I get to combine venues, eras, and calendars. And I get to use my Hebrew name, which means Benjamin the Wolf.

My given name, Gregg David Bordowitz, isn't the same as my Hebrew name. That's not uncommon, at least among Queens-bred Ashkenazis whose parents inscribed every child's birth certificate with the ambition to become American—and, specifically, to raise a tennis-playing, gin-and-tonic-drinking cardiologist with a *gorgeous* view of Central Park. Don't believe me? Ask my best friend from grade school, Randall Lautenberg, who somehow was never mistaken for a member of the House of Windsor.

At temple, if your name is Martin, you're called Moshe; if your name is Harold, you're called Herschel. When I'm at temple—when I'm not in surgery—and I have the honor of being asked to read from the Torah, the rabbi calls on Benjamin the Wolf. Pretty cool, I think. Better than calling on Gregg David Bordowitz, right?

I'm not a comedian, in case you haven't noticed. I'm an artist who plays a comedian in museums. Being an artist, though, is similar to being a failed comedian. For a long time, I've felt that, in our culture, being a *fine* artist—which is how I like to think of myself, when I'm in a stable psychological state—is like being a failed comedian. The jokes don't land; no one gets it.

I really, really identify with the person at the open mic night who isn't famous, doesn't have many friends in the audience, and isn't getting *any* laughs. It's abject. For me, of course, the abjection is constant—no audience necessary!

If you want to be a failed comedian, you might as well be an artist. And if you're going to be an artist, you might as well save on storage fees by bringing your library on the road.

[*Points to the books and other objects on shelves on the stage.*]

These beloved books constitute my research for the show—and, I suppose, they constitute myself: the Talmud (English, Hebrew, and Aramaic), Moses ben Jacob Cordovero's *Or Ne'erav*, Abraham Joshua Heschel's *God in Search of Man*, Stuart Hall's *The Fateful Triangle*, Lenny Bruce's *How to Talk Dirty and Influence People*, Michael Gold's *Jews Without Money*, Henry Roth's *Call It Sleep,* Lauren Berlant's *Cruel Optimism*, and on and on. Prepare for footnotes!

I wanted the set to have a wandering-Jew-unpacking-his-library feel. I don't own this stage, but I want you to feel like I do, like you're trapped inside my head. Like you're ... me. I've got my siddur, and my tallis bag, which I take to shul. I've got a sign printed with an image of the *etz chaim*—the tree of life—copied from one that Cordovero made in the 1500s. And there's the symbol behind me, on the poster board: a rendering of the tree that looks like a slice of the trunk, with the rings taking the shape of letters. Each of the ten lines is composed from the first letter of the word for one of the ten *sefirot*, or attributes of G-d, which also form the points on the tree.

Of course, I've got a bottle of Manischewitz, which is a nod to the culture of the 1950s and '60s. Same goes for my socks. The biggest wardrobe decision I had to make for this show was whether to wear black or white socks. I wore white as a tribute to Jerry Lewis. Otherwise, I'm not doing costumes; I'm not dressing up like a rock star, rabbi, or comedian. I do, however, bear a striking resemblance to Shelley Berman—one of the "sick comedians"—on the cover of his first LP, *Outside Shelley Berman*, the best-selling comedy album of 1959.

Take a look at the cover.

[*Holds up the LP, with the cover facing the audience.*]

Now look at me. Look at my suit.

[*Looks down and examines his suit, which is plain but sharp, with a modern, slim cut and narrow lapels.*]

This is exactly how he dressed; this is how he looked. Actually, all the "sick comedians" dressed like this: Berman, Lenny Bruce, Mort Sahl, Allan Sherman, and so on. All the Jewish stand-up acts in Greenwich Village in the 1960s wore the same suit. Why? I guess you had to look professional. You had to look like you were fulfilling your parents' dream of ascending to the middle class, like you'd moved out of Queens, like you weren't desperately cashing in on your ethnicity.

My family was always listening to albums by comedians, especially Borscht Belt figures like Buddy Hackett and Shecky Greene. Lenny Bruce was a legend by name, but I never got to listen to him as a child, despite my parents being huge fans of benign neglect. I had to get Bruce's albums for myself when I was a teenager; I'd borrow or steal records by him, Richard Pryor, and Steve Martin. Word would spread that a friend—or a friend's older brother or cousin—had an album, and we'd figure out whose parents weren't home, head over, get high, and laugh our asses off. If the parents were home, we'd stuff towels under the door, smoke a joint, then fumigate the room with Lysol. Just like in the movies.

I found Lenny Bruce's *The Midnight Concert* at a store in Long Island that had punk records. British imports! I listened to that album over and over and over again. Bruce's attitude and style made him the godfather of punk, in my eyes. He thought and spoke at a higher velocity than everyone else; he embraced the freedom of improvisation; he used dirty words; and he wasn't afraid to perform to type, to come across as *too* Jewish. In fact, he flaunted his identity, he rubbed his Jewishness in the face of his audience.

Why were Bruce and his cohort called the "sick comedians"? Because, to critics in the late 1950s, they came across as mentally unstable. To fans of McCarthyism, they seemed to be symptomatic of the sickness of the culture, like the Beats. The "sickniks" weren't showmen out to please the audience and get laughs; they were mining Jewish neurosis, testing the limits of comedy, and making people uncomfortable. They were cutting, profane, and confrontational.

The sick comedians, in other words, were a cross between my grandmother and the Ramones. They embodied—and exaggerated—the idiom in which I grew up. They played pathological versions of the standard stereotypes. Think of Woody Allen's stand-up persona: the high-strung, maladjusted, self-loathing Jew. Mort Sahl, on the other hand, was all about being too smart for his own good, too far to the left for comfort. He moved from headline to headline, skewering the government and calling out hypocrisy.

And Lenny Bruce? All of the above. He was known for his foul mouth, of course: he was arrested for saying "cocksucker," "tits and ass," and—I'll never get over this—"schmuck." But he broke with the conventions of language in another way: he used Yiddish in his routines, and he refused to translate the Yiddish into English. He was unabashedly Jewish, but he was also obnoxiously masculine. He was an affront to the idea that Jewish men were weak or effeminate. He was not your typical *feygele*!

(I might say the same of myself.)

Bruce went further: he took on the role—the anti-Semitic trope—of the Jewish pervert. By enacting the transgression on stage, he got rid of the shame associated with sexual fantasies, sexual deviance. If I were a psychologist, I might say that he cultivated a counterphobic attitude.

And, of course, during his discourses on perversion, oral sex, bestiality, civil rights, STDs, Barry Goldwater, drugs, female anatomy, racism, free speech, corrupt cops, and white ethnics, Bruce admitted, over and over again, that the Jews killed Christ—which, in my experience as a schoolchild, was not a joke. Here's a version of the "We Killed Christ" bit:

> In the dictionary, a Jew is one who is descended from the ancient tribe of Judea. But ... you and I know what a Jew is: one who killed our lord. I don't know if we got much press on that in Illinois—we did this about two thousand years ago. Two thousand years of Polack kids whacking the shit out of us coming home from school. Dear, dear. And although there should be a statute of limitations for that crime, it seems that those who neither have the actions nor the gait of Christians, pagans or not, will bust us out—unrelenting dues for another deuce.
>
> I really searched it out—why we pay the dues. Why do you keep breaking our balls for this crime?

> "Why, Jew, because you skirt the issue. You blame it on the Roman soldiers."
>
> Alright, I'll clear the air once and for all and confess. Yes, we did it. I did it—my family. I found a note in my basement. It said: "We killed him." Signed: Morty.
>
> A lot of people say to me, "Why did you kill Christ?"
>
> "I dunno. It was one of those parties ... got out of hand, you know?"
>
> We killed him because he didn't want to become a doctor; that's why we killed him.

To me, Bruce originated the punk disposition. He was revolutionary: he didn't do one-liners, he didn't care about being funny. His life became the act, but he never really revealed himself. He didn't turn to autobiography, like Pryor. He was a hipster; he was always a little opaque, like he was hiding something.

But how's Bruce remembered? As a First Amendment case and a proto–Howard Stern who died of an overdose. And the other sick comedians? Sahl was a self-proclaimed bohemian who disavowed the "craft" of comedy—the banality of the one-liner—in favor of jazz-inspired improvisations. But he's remembered as the progressive Jew of the Johnny Carson galaxy. You can go on YouTube and watch him be reduced to innocuous political jokes about Nixon and Kissinger being liars and murderers.

Fortunately, I don't have to do the work of restoring the reputations of these comedians. Films have been made, and they're available on Netflix. Biographies: Amazon. Dissertations: JSTOR. I do, however, have to reject the idea that the sick comedians were merely channeling the anxieties of the age, allowing audiences to laugh off the threat of nuclear war and stifling conformity, like Cold War–era Jimmy Kimmels. They were not using humor as a release. They were expressing aggression!

As a kid, that's how I saw humor: a vehicle for anger, resentment, and alienation. I grew up hearing comedians channel all of these feelings, all of these experiences of anti-Semitism. The humor of the sick comedians was the lingua franca of my childhood. To survive in my family, you had to be sharp; you had to absorb constant insults, and you had to be ready with stinging comebacks. We, too, were sick. Very sick.

For most of my life, I've been preoccupied with the nature, function, and form of jokes. I've been obsessed with humor, especially Jewish humor. What is Jewish humor? I'll tell you a Jewish joke and then we'll figure out why it's funny. Here we go: a math teacher is teaching a room of grade-school kids. He asks, "What's 2 percent?" A Jewish kid raises his hand and says, "You're right!"

[*Silence from the audience.*]

You don't have to laugh! I think that's a hysterical joke, but I took a while to figure it out. How does the joke work? Basically, it's a rhetorical-question joke. What's 2 percent? The answer is *bubkes* or *gor nisht*—nothing. That's the real answer. Two percent on the back end of a deal is ... *nothing*, right? The Jewish kid understands this, he agrees: to him, the question has to be rhetorical. That's the joke—not that the kid's cheap. If your interpretation is that the kid's cheap, well, you're probably anti-Semitic.

[*Laughter from the audience.*]

Now you're laughing! If you're laughing because you understand the importance of the rhetorical question in Jewish thought, then you're probably Jewish. If you're laughing because you understand business acumen as endemic to the Jewish people—and conspicuous even in the behavior of grade-school kids—then you're probably anti-Semitic.

All Jewish jokes reveal how Jews joke about themselves, which means that all Jewish jokes can be understood as anti-Semitic. Whether the joke lands as insulting, self-critical, or even self-revelatory depends on the disposition of the audience in relation to the joke. What I mean is: Jews and neo-Nazis love Jewish jokes for the same reason.

I could be on stage in front of an audience of people like you or people with MAGA hats; either way, I could tell Jewish jokes all night and bring down the house. But I'm not really going for laughs—that much is clear.

What am I going for? I'm trying to sketch out how humor changes based on how I understand myself and how the audience understands me. Am I an insider or outsider? What about you? Do I want you to laugh or squirm? If I tell a joke about Jews, does that make the joke Jewish?

What's the test case? Holocaust humor, obviously. The existence of Auschwitz jokes shows that nothing is so traumatic or terrible as to be off limits, especially to Jews. But there's a difference between gallows humor and executioner's humor, between Jews telling jokes in order to deal with fear and oppression and Germans telling jokes in order to dehumanize Jews.

In other words: Jews don't really joke about the Holocaust. Once, I was telling Jewish jokes to someone I was dating—someone who was not Jewish—and they said, "I know a Jewish joke!"

"Oh, really! What Jewish joke do you know?"

"Well, how do you fit a thousand Jews into a Volkswagen?"

I don't need to tell you the punch line. You've probably heard a version of the joke—which is *not* Jewish—or come across the theme of Jews being reduced to ashes. I don't know where the joke originated, but I've read about the connection between the Jews-in-a-Volkswagen line and German anti-Semites. Surprise!

A while ago, I told the Volkswagen joke on stage as part of a performance. Why? I felt like the audience wasn't appreciating the distinction between laughing at Jewish humor and laughing at Jews. I might have been projecting. But I decided to test them by telling what is clearly an anti-Semitic joke. After the performance, I felt sick. I thought, "How could I possibly have repeated that racist joke in the service of a performance?"

The joke worked, though. The audience got my point. And that made me hate myself even more. I was spiraling. Then, after the performance, some Israelis who'd been in the audience came up to me. I was very sheepish and apologetic. "I was worried about the Volkswagen joke—it's terrible," I said.

"Oh, we've been hearing that joke since we were seven," one of them replied. Because there are so many survivors in Israel—and because Jews are Jews—they'd grown up with unfathomably bleak Holocaust humor. Apparently, the Ashkenazis in

Israel had turned anti-Semitic jokes into Jewish jokes.

We had a discussion about coming of age in the wake of the Holocaust. I'd grown up in a Jewish neighborhood in Queens, surrounded by people who'd fled anti-Semitism in Europe, lost family and friends in the Holocaust, and survived the camps. No one I knew would tell a Holocaust joke! My family had a very serious sense of inside versus outside, which had to do with the extraordinary level of prejudice in the United States. Jokes about Jews were for Jews; if they made fun of Jews, they did so with love. Jewish humor was an expression of the anxiety of conforming to type—an expression of the tension between being Jewish and becoming American.

I remember being with my family after Yom Kippur services when I was eleven or twelve, at the Orthodox temple where I was bar mitzvahed. We were walking around, visiting other families, which is what you do. And we saw, down the street, Max Rosenberg, smoking a cigarette. Max was the *shammash* at our Orthodox temple: the helper, the one who sings louder and earlier than everybody else, to keep them in time. He and his wife, Yetta, a seamstress, were the first people I met who had serial numbers from the concentration camps tattooed on their arms. You're not supposed to smoke a cigarette on *yontif*. And this might've even been one of those special occasions when Shabbos and Yom Kippur fell on the same day. But Max was smoking. He saw us and put the cigarette behind his back. We stopped and said, "Good *yontif*. May you be inscribed."

Max was talking to us and the cigarette was burning, burning, burning. We could see the smoke rising above his head. But he wasn't going to smoke in front of us. I must've been eight or nine, and I thought to myself: *What kind of G-d is this? Let him smoke! Let. Him. Smoke.*

[*Laughter.*]

I don't know if that's funny! It's a difficult story to tell.

Many of us—not only Jews—enjoy self-loathing, but the jokes we tell about ourselves aren't meant to justify persecution. Ultimately, the jokes that Gentiles tell about Jews tend to serve that purpose: they act as an outlet for expressing animosity, for belittling and marginalizing us. When we tell jokes about ourselves, we can't help but reproduce some of that aggression. But Jewish jokes about money aren't about Jews being rich, they're about Jews being poor. We're cheap because we're poor, not because we're hoarding money!

The modern Jewish joke originated with the Depression: the preoccupation with not having money and, later, the preoccupation with new money. Jewish comedy emerged with a generation that experienced serious poverty, compounded by prejudice, even as they were pushed to assimilate, to become doctors and lawyers, to move to the suburbs. Figures like Bruce, Sahl, and Berman transmuted that experience into comedy, which was also a way of differentiating themselves from the previous generation, from the Borscht Belt humor that'd entertained their parents.

Here's Berman—real name, Sheldon—drawing the line in "Conversation with My Father," from his 1959 album:

> My father owned the delicatessen downstairs. This is the West Side of Chicago, an almost exclusively Jewish neighborhood. Here we thrive—lowering real estate values. [*Laughter.*] And here we are moderately happy because we do not know from such things and we couldn't help it anyway. [*Laughter.*] My father makes a reasonably good living in his delicatessen selling sandwiches to the laborers in the neighborhood, and there are many laborers in this neighborhood. My father refers to laborers in a rather peculiar fashion: he calls them ... *goyim*. [*Laughter.*] I will explain this esoteric term—nobody will be let down, I assure you. *Goyim* is plural for *goy*. [*Laughter.*] *Goy* is a rather singular way of saying gentile. As far as my father is concerned, all laborers are gentiles. [*Laughter.*] Even

> a Jew who is a laborer is a gentile, as far as my father is concerned. [*Laughter.*] He is an *exceedingly* narrow-minded man.

Berman was anxious, harsh, and cutting in his observations about daily life, especially the moments of humiliation, awkwardness, and frustration. But he was different from the rest. He never left his stool while performing, which made him seem more like a drummer than a comedian. He told stories about Jewish neurosis, but he hardly talked like the person whose foibles and failures he was recounting; he had such a gentle voice, and his delivery was so easygoing, that he seemed to be describing a patient he was seeing. Listening to his albums, I felt like *he* was listening to *me*.

I needed someone to listen to me! I needed a reformed rabbi who dabbled in psychoanalysis. I was under a lot of pressure to make something of myself, and I absorbed my family's shame about failing to climb the ladder. Our friends and relatives professionalized and moved to New Rochelle, while we were stuck in Queens. Stuck in a Philip Roth novel. My grandmother didn't go to high school, my grandfather didn't go to college, and my parents didn't go to college. My grandfather was a laborer at a clock factory in Flatiron. My stepfather worked for a speaker manufacturer and my mother moved between retail jobs.

We were Jews without money. We were among the many thousands of Jews who arrived in the United States with nothing and found work, had families, fought in wars, harbored ambitions, but, somehow, never got to the middle class. I used to hear about kids having incredible, lavish bar mitzvahs. But I never went to any of them until I was fourteen, when I got a job with a photographer shooting bar mitzvahs and weddings in Long Island. One time, we were shooting at an enormous banquet hall—grandparents dancing with teenagers, parents hitting on each other's spouses and raiding the buffet—and, suddenly, the walls on one end slid open. There was another half of the space, which was set up like a Las Vegas casino: craps, card tables with dealers, and a monumental roulette wheel. The dealers passed out fake hundred-dollar bills with the boy's *punim* in place of Ben Franklin's. Everyone got wasted; the kid was stuffing cash in every pocket and showering his friends with bills.

How were the bar mitzvahs in my neighborhood? Mom made chopped liver for thirty people. We did have wads of cash: relatives handed them to the thirteen-year-olds as if they were paying protection money. Some kids made thousands of dollars! I think I got thirteen hundred dollars, which went to covering our rent.

[*Laughter.*]

Not a joke! My parents were having trouble that month.

[*Laughter.*]

I guess there's something funny about not being funny?

[*Laughter dies down.*]

These days, you don't hear so many Jewish—or gentile—comedians telling jokes about Jews and money. Jews in the United States are experiencing a moment of assimilation, which encourages us to forget our past, to act as if we were never marginalized or demonized. But we do have a past: we were poor and fixated on money; we were selling sandwiches and lowering real-estate values; we were Holocaust survivors handing out cash at bar mitzvahs in Queens. We were "kikes."

I didn't grow up with much anti-Semitism, but I got called "kike" here and there. I never hear the word anymore, except from my friend Steve, a brilliant, lovable nebbish who happens to be sitting in the front row. Whenever I'm being cheap about going to a restaurant, Steve says, "Don't be such a kike!" I love when Steve says that to me. He understands that Jews didn't always have money, and that the vast majority of Jews are not rich. He understands that Jews aren't plotting to steal the jobs of *real* Americans. And he understands the tenuousness and superficiality of assimilation. At any moment, we could become kikes again. Perhaps that's already happening. Perhaps, at least, we should act as if that's already happening.

I've been thinking about this—about the myth of assimilation—since the neo-Nazis marched in Charlottesville in 2017, chanting, "Jews will not replace us." When I first saw the coverage—bands of white men wearing polo shirts, hoisting torches, and doing Nazi salutes—I didn't understand what was going on. I actually googled "Jews will not replace us." I read newspaper articles about white nationalists charging Jews with transforming the demography of the country by—somehow—jacking up the birth rates of minorities and engineering an assault on our borders by immigrants. Suddenly, I felt like I was a Jew in medieval times, accused of orchestrating a global conspiracy to take over the economy (even though my parents used my bar mitzvah money to pay rent). I was a party to *The Protocols of the Elders of Zion*. I was a kike—and not because I didn't want to spend twenty-five dollars on a plate of grilled chicken.

After Charlottesville, like an angry, aggressive Moshe, I said: I'm going to take my queer, communist, Jewish ass on the road and spout Yiddish in front of people who don't really understand what I'm saying!

Sounds funny, right? And it works! Wait, wait—watch: *rachmones*.

[*Laughter.*]

I thought you'd laugh. Jewish humor is easy: all you have to do, in most parts of the country, is be Jewish. None of this is scripted! I'm just being Jewish.

Getting people to laugh by making fun of myself—for speaking a "gutter" language, for being cheap, for being helpless without psychoanalysis—may be easy, but, as I said, that's not what I'm after. That's not what Lenny Bruce was after. People say that Bruce wasn't all that funny, but I don't think the point of comedy is to get laughs. And if that *is* the point, I have to ask: Why are we laughing? To what end?

[*Looks to the audience; silence.*]

Laughter is the best medicine, right?

I'm sorry, I'm sorry. I'm sure Patch Adams was a wonderful doctor. But there's a difference between watching comedy to get over a bout of depression and relying on memes and late-night shows to deal with dehumanization, corruption, inequality, and so on. *We have to keep laughing until the whole Trump nightmare is over!* That's what we're told; that's what the networks want us to believe; that's what the algorithms direct us to do. Why, though? We're not soldiers attending a USO show, right? We're citizens living under the threat of authoritarianism.

I don't object to laughing. But I don't think comedy is necessarily good for us.

Is comedy good for us?

[*Prolonged silence.*]

Sorry—you were just laughing, and you might laugh again soon. I'm not chiding you for laughing! I just think there are many different reasons to laugh, not all of them having to do with humor. Laughter is not identical to humor. We often laugh involuntarily—not because of a joke, but to express disbelief, defiance, or scorn.

Laughter is fundamental, but that doesn't mean humor is curative. That doesn't mean we get through hard times by telling jokes, by distracting or unburdening ourselves. We don't deal with political crises by making jokes.

There are a lot of theories of humor that suggest otherwise. You can go back to medieval carnivals and claim humor as a "weapon of the weak."

You can celebrate jokes that make us realize how ridiculous—and changeable—everything is. You can quote Orwell: "Every joke is a tiny revolution." *You* can; not me. I don't have a theory of humor. I don't think it's possible to comprehend humor. Humor causes a break in understanding, an aporia. Humor also causes an opening.

The comedy that's worthy of being broadcast on television, though, tends to be easily subsumed by the market, which is why the humor having to do with Trump—with Trump's fascism—was very quickly exhausted. The late-night hosts, however heartfelt, are selling a product: anti-Trumpism. When I watch the monologues skewering Trump, I can't help but imagine the focus groups. I can't help but think that we're laughing instead of facing the facts: the nightmare isn't just going to end, the crisis isn't just going to disappear.

Nevertheless, I watch the shows. I try to laugh. But then I wake up the next day and read the newspaper: *How else can we distract them? Let's see ... how about we do away with needle-exchange programs? How about we give $8 billion to ICE, an unaccountable fascist organization that criminalizes immigrants and bolsters white supremacy? How about we take $20 million away from the Ryan White Program, a thirty-year-old vehicle for funding care for people with HIV/*

AIDS, and give that money to ICE to help cover the cost of separating children from their parents and detaining them in warehouses in the desert without access to phones or doctors?

Where's the fucking punch line?

More and more, the scales are falling from my eyes: Trump has been turned into material to boost ratings, to sell advertising. That doesn't have to be the case. Think of Jon Stewart when he was doing *The Daily Show*, before Trump. He was brilliant—he was like Karl Kraus, the famous Austrian intellectual who published, edited, and wrote nearly every word in *Die Fackel* (The Torch), the antifascist, pacifist newspaper. From 1911 until 1936, when Kraus died, *Die Fackel* assailed the corruption and hypocrisy of Austrian society, and mercilessly made fun of every other newspaper in the German-speaking world.

Kraus was a master of aphorisms: "Things are happening that could not be imagined and ... what can no longer be imagined must happen, for if one could imagine it, it would not happen." He's no Jimmy Kimmel, but he's not bad, right? How about this one: "Through decades of practice, [the reporter] has produced in mankind that degree of unimaginativeness which enables it to wage a war of extermination against itself."

The syntax, I realize, isn't ready for late night. But that's why Jon Stewart was so great: he was Kraus with a middle-class background, Gen X sensibility, and New Jersey patois. He was the Kraus of his day. And he was, of course, born as Jonathan Stuart Leibowitz.

Now we have comedians who rely on Trump for material, whose routines are all about repeating what he says with a smirk or sneer, as if that makes his racism and fascism funny or innocuous. They've become enormously popular and successful thanks to Trump. They've been delegated to express the despair and disgust of millions of viewers, but they've also normalized Trump by making his behavior seem routine. Their routines are his routine. If I were Stephen Colbert, who's smart—or Jimmy Kimmel, who's kind of smart—or Jimmy Fallon, who's ... I don't know. Who's Jimmy Fallon? That's a good one: Who's Jimmy Fallon? Do you understand that as a rhetorical joke? If so, you're Jewish.

To be honest, I only watch the late-night shows when I'm traveling. I'm living in the present, of course, so I don't have a television, I have a laptop. But when I'm in a hotel room, I'm within three feet of a big-ass television. I go back to being a child at the Bordowitz household in Kew Gardens, circa 1974, watching basic cable and eating half-frozen kugel. Often, in those moments—as I chew on exorbitant macadamia nuts, watch Jimmy Kimmel grin and chuckle while repeating Trump's latest blasphemies, and feel disgusted with myself—I think about the status of the joke and the status of the question. I might even turn off the TV and pick up *God in Search of Man*, by Abraham Joshua Heschel, the great Polish rabbi and theologian, who fled the Nazis and spent the rest of his life in New York City.

[*Removes book from a shelf on the stage, holds it up for the audience to see.*]

Heschel says that religion is a "sublime answer," but we no longer know the question that's being asked, so we can't understand the Bible. We have to stop focusing on the answer—doctrine—and start asking questions about the nature of existence.

Lenny Bruce didn't deliver answers. He didn't do punch lines. He didn't tell people how to understand the world. Instead, he pointed to the limits of understanding. There's a joke about Jews answering questions with questions, and the joke is true: a question always leads to another question; knowledge always exists under a veil of doubt. That's the humility of Jewish thought.

I've spent my entire life asking questions. Believe me, I haven't gotten many answers. And why should

I have? To me, what's important is properly forming and constantly reframing the questions—which is what we're doing tonight: questions, digressions, questions. Heschel describes philosophy as "the art of asking the right questions" and his work as a "quest for forgotten questions." The question is the condition for the answer being comprehensible, meaningful, and powerful. Heschel writes:

> There are dead thoughts and there are living thoughts. A dead thought has been compared to a stone which one may plant in the soil. Nothing will come out. A living thought is like a seed. In the process of thinking, an answer without a question is devoid of life. It may enter the mind; it will not penetrate the soul. It may become a part of one's knowledge; it will not come forth as a creative force.

When I'm not watching late-night shows—when I'm not reading Heschel—I'm tuning in to *Seinfeld*. Every evening, at every hotel in the country, *Seinfeld* is on. *Seinfeld* will be on air until long after I'm dead, until televisions go the way of phone booths.

I started watching *Seinfeld* when the show debuted in 1989, and I fell in love. A show about Jews in New York! I never cared for Jerry Seinfeld's stand-up routines, but for the purposes of the show, his character—a conventional, smug, craft-obsessed comedian—was perfect. From the start, though, I was uncomfortable with the representation of other ethnicities: there were all of these characters with absurd accents, as if the foreignness was the joke.

Each week, I'd get together with a group of friends, all of whom happened to be Jewish, and watch *Seinfeld*. We were fascinated by the displays of Jewish racism, but we were more focused on the depiction of Jews on television. We talked a lot about the *The Munsters* and *The Addams Family*, which we thought were about different kinds of Jewish families.

One dear friend, Richard Elovich, a performer and fellow AIDS activist, brought this debate into his one-man show *Someone Else from Queens Is Queer* in 1991. The performer is recounting his effort to get his lover to sleep with him and stop analyzing the two sitcoms:

> "Herman and Lily Munster come from an entirely different class. They are like us, from Queens. Herman Munster is different from Gomez Addams. Herman is constantly seeking to assimilate. The happiest I have ever seen Herman is in the episode where he has won, in a TV contest, a month's free membership in the Mockingbird Heights Country Club! So he and Lily go to this country club and totally fuck up! Misunderstand everything!"
>
> Gordie's taking his clothes off.
>
> "See, no matter what Herman Munster does, no matter how much he tries to sound like 'Father Knows Best,' he has that nose! That face! He always looks like

Frankenstein!"

I run for the pillows and the sheets.

"The difference is Gomez Addams can pass, and that's all the more interesting because he doesn't know he's passing."

I turn out the light.

"The Jewish dream vision of aristocracy..."

We get into bed.

"Not ever remembering a time when one wasn't aristocracy!"

You could tell, as a kid, if your family was more like the Munsters or the Addams: working-class Jews desperate to become middle-class Americans (Munsters) or pretentious Jews who couldn't let go of the aristocratic world they'd left behind (Addams).

Seinfeld is totally different: the show is a comedy *of* Jewish racism. That racism is what follows—and enables—assimilation. Somehow, I had to watch *Seinfeld* for thousands of hours to realize that the entire basis of the show is a group of Jews making fun of people who are Black and brown, people with accents. The characters have become white, so they skewer people who aren't white, people who lack power and status. The result? Jerry and his pals are really satisfied with themselves! After all, they benefit from the social order being reinforced.

No wonder Steve Bannon made millions on the syndication rights! *Seinfeld* is one of the greatest testaments to the consolidation of whiteness—and to Jewish complicity. I'll break it down: Seinfeld is Jewish. Kramer—*come on*. George Costanza has an Italian name, but have you seen his parents? He's a Juido, basically. (Takes one to know one.) And Elaine Benes: she's the daughter of a writer; she's a Five Colleges Jew, right? She probably went to Hampshire. So we've got four Jews in leading roles. And what do they do? They make fun of how Pakistanis talk.

Remember "The Red Dot," the episode where George is sleeping with the immigrant who cleans the office? He gives her a cashmere sweater—discounted because of a stain—to keep her quiet, because of "Clarence Thomas and everything." Then comes the caricature: the cleaner's soliloquy about being a "little girl in Panama" and begging a rich American for the cashmere sweater off his back.

Why'd I take thirty years to recognize *Seinfeld* as the epitome of Jewish racism? Why'd I keep laughing?

This questions brings to mind Hannah Gadsby's stand-up show *Nanette*, which involves a story about being beaten by a homophobic person at a bus stop: Gadsby tells a joke about the incident, leaving out the violence, and everyone laughs. Then, later,

Gadsby reveals what really happened, and no one laughs. The joke only works, Gadsby explains, if the audience gets to relate to the queer comedian—and laugh at the stupid homophobe—rather than reckon with trauma. I hadn't seen someone so naked on stage since Pryor's *Live on the Sunset Strip*, which hinges on him turning the fear of being lynched—and the story of freebasing cocaine, setting himself on fire, going to the hospital, and nearly dying—into comedy. He challenges the audience to laugh, and to ask themselves why they're laughing.

I've thought about Pryor and Gadsby as I've asked why I took so long to realize the extent of the racism on *Seinfeld*. My impression of the show had to do with the history of Jewish racism—the racism of my childhood, my family, my community, and the comedy albums that I listened to when I was a kid. I listened to Buddy Hackett, who, in his most famous bit, imitates a Chinese waiter: he adopts an absurd, incomprehensible accent and goes over the choices on the menu, telling the diners that they can or can't have one or three dishes from "corumn A" in combination with two or four dishes from "corumn B," and so on. He gets the order wrong—or the diners fail to interpret the menu—over and over again; he insults and sexually harasses the diners; he says ... "flied lice."

[*Audience groans.*]

How many of you know this routine?

[*Looks to the audience, registers raised hands.*]

A few people. I'm sorry. I'm really sorry. Everyone else: listen to Hackett's 1960 album *The Original Chinese Waiter.* Or, actually, don't—please don't. The bit is really, really racist. And the family listening to the waiter, trying to figure out what he's saying, is my own, basically: a Jewish family in Queens that goes for Chinese food once a week.

What's the difference between *Seinfeld*'s racism and Hackett's racism? Or my grandfather's racism? He grew up on the Lower East Side in the 1920s and '30s, the youngest of six siblings in a Yiddish-speaking household. At the time, every block in the area was defined by race and ethnicity. If you were on the wrong block at the wrong time, serious damage could be done to you. My grandfather left the neighborhood to fight in World War II, which encouraged him to be prejudiced against Asians. After the war, he developed the double consciousness that went along with growing up as a Jew, then experiencing the transformation of Jews into white people, which granted some privileges. He was a liberal Democrat, in favor of civil rights, but he had no concept of disidentifying with his own racism.

I don't forgive my grandfather's racism—racism is racism. But my grandfather was a lovely guy, and I never noticed him treating people differently based on race. I always looked past the Jewish racism of the 1950s and '60s because Jews were marching in Alabama and getting murdered while registering Black voters in Mississippi. What can I say? I grew up with a romantic view of Jews as allies, as key players in the civil rights movement. I grew up with the image of Heschel marching with Martin Luther King in Selma—"praying with my feet," as he said.

In New York and other cities, though, Jews and Black people gradually parted ways, to put it lightly. Why? Landlordism and Palestine. But no one I knew talked much about this—or about the exploitation of Black people by Jews, the racism directed at Black people by Jews—until the riots in my neighborhood, Crown Heights, in 1991. An Orthodox Jewish driver ran into and killed a seven-year-old Black boy, then a group of teenagers stabbed and killed a Jew, then the neighborhood exploded.

Where's the punch line? Ask Seinfeld. His show was on as the riots were happening, as the divide between Jews and Black people was being exposed. But Jerry, George, Elaine, and Kramer never got the news; they kept on skewering unnamed Black and brown characters for thwarting them, upstaging them, humiliating them, and policing them. I guess there was nothing funny—or nothing transformative—about the riots.

There's a through line, right? *Seinfeld* didn't come from nowhere. Nevertheless, I can't help but defend my grandfather by trying to understand his racism, the racism of the world I grew up in. I don't intend to gloss over the contradictions; I don't want to ignore the tension between Black and Jewish populations, or turn Jews into civil rights kitsch. But there's a difference between Buddy Hackett and Jerry Seinfeld, which has to do with the thirty years between them. Hackett's Chinese waiter bit—that's about the relationship between Jews and Chinese people, competing immigrant groups.

No!?! Am I making a distinction without a difference? I realize that *Seinfeld* and Hackett are part of the story of the consolidation of whiteness in the United States over the course of a century. And ... racism is racism, right?

Even so, the racism of every era *is* different. Today, Jews in the United States appear to be white to nearly everyone—everyone except for the people carrying torches and chanting, "Jews will not replace us." The neo-Nazis wouldn't be surprised to learn that, when my ancestors came to this country, they got papers identifying them as members of the

Hebrew race. A hundred years later, though, Jews are white. A hundred years later, we have Seth Rogen!

How did Jews become white? And, having become white, why do they still feel the need to perform ethnicity as a mode of entertainment? Why does Seth Rogen sport a Jewfro? In *Knocked Up*, he's dancing with Katherine Heigl's character, who runs her hand through his hair and says, "I love your curly hair! It's so great. Do you, like, use product or anything?" And he replies, "I use, uh—'Jew,' it's called."

Why?!? His act isn't counterphobic; he's not a sick comedian. *No one* can be a sick comedian in the age of Seth Rogen.

I get angry at Jewish comics for pretending that assimilation in the United States is easy and always has been easy, as if difference can be reduced to a Jewfro. This is a pet peeve of mine. What do they think life was like for people like my grandfather? He couldn't attend Columbia because of the quotas. He couldn't join a country club. He couldn't join a standard secret society; he had to settle for a Jewish fraternal order, the Knights of Pythias. He always remembered going to the South for basic training and seeing signs that said: "No Jews and Blacks and Dogs Allowed."

Well, Seth, it's not 1950: you can get into the country club. You can own the country club.

I have nothing against Seth Rogen. He's actually very funny. But when I think of Rogen and his Jewfro, my mind goes to Bernie Madoff, Harvey Weinstein, and Roy Cohn. I can't help but ask the age-old question: is it good for the Jews? The Jews were not happy about Madoff, Weinstein, or Cohn. (No Jewish parent in my neighborhood ever told a child, "You could grow up to be the next Roy Cohn!") Yet these men are paragons of assimilation—of the status, wealth, and power that Jews, having become white, can attain. At the same time, they're representatives of the rootless cosmopolitans, targets of Stormfront and the Proud Boys, and characters in *The Protocols of the Elders of Zion*, which is more popular now than ever. Jews like Madoff, Weinstein, and Cohn participate in the consolidation of whiteness, but they never—or never fully—become white.

So why am *I* performing my ethnicity? Well, the question is better than the answer. And the answer is in the medium.

Cue the music.

> We're a happy family
> We're a happy family
> We're a happy family
> Me, Mom, and Dad
> We're a happy family
> We're a happy family

We're a happy family
Me, Mom, and Dad

Sitting here in Queens
Eating refried beans
We're in all the magazines
Gulpin' down Thorazines
We ain't got no friends
Our troubles never end
No Christmas cards to send
Daddy likes men

Daddy's telling lies
Baby's eating flies
Mommy's on pills
Baby's got the chills

I'm friends with the President
I'm friends with the Pope
We're all making a fortune
Selling Daddy's dope

Sitting here in Queens
Eating refried beans
We're in all the magazines
Gulpin' down Thorazines
We ain't got no friends
Our troubles never end
No Christmas cards to send
Daddy likes men

The Ramones come from my homeland, Queens. Joey and Tommy were Jews, as was the manager, Danny. "We're a Happy Family" is a portrait of a Queens household not unlike my own.

How many of you can relate? Did you sit at the dinner table and repeat to yourself, "We're a happy family, we're a happy family, we're a happy family"? Can I get a witness?

I went from my family's dinner table in Queens to CBGB. I moved to Manhattan soon after the Ramones started playing at the downtown clubs, dressed in matching leather jackets and jeans. They weren't trying to be clever or sophisticated: they were outer-borough kids with bad haircuts and clothes held together with safety pins, playing three-chord songs and rhyming "Queens" with "beans." They embraced stupidity, which is why I loved them.

Maybe now this is lost on people, but in the 1980s, there was virtue in being stupid. Reagan was in the White House, then Bush. The culture offered us nothing. The notion of striving for recognition, impressing the gatekeepers, and eventually entering the mainstream seemed completely ridiculous. We were making our own culture—at the A7 club, the Roxy, the Pyramid Club, and Danceteria. Our lives depended on us being outsiders.

These days, the question I'm asking myself is: what does it mean to be an American artist? The Ramones were true American artists. They turned being outsiders into a performance. They embodied the type: anonymous, impenetrable, unattractive, yet somehow brilliant, magnetic, and universal. Patti Smith said, in the 1970s, "At heart, I am an American artist, and I have no guilt." Ironically, she's revised her opinion: she recently said, "I'm an American artist and I feel guilty about everything." So, I suppose, she's now a Jewish American artist?

Allen Ginsberg is an American artist—and a rock star, a rabbi, a comedian. The most important line of poetry I've read in my life is from "Howl": "America I'm putting my queer shoulder to the wheel." I used to idolize Ginsberg. When I was nineteen, I went up to him after a reading to ask a question. I wanted to ask him the hardest question—I got that from Hebrew school. I always had to ask *the* question, which I'd spend most of class formulating. The other kids hated me for that. But I didn't learn my lesson until Ginsberg shot me down.

What did I say? Not, "Mr. Ginsberg, I love you." Not, "Mr. Ginsberg, you changed my life." Nothing like that. I said, "Mr. Ginsberg, how did Jack Kerouac expect to achieve satori when he was drinking so much?"

Ginsberg was pissed! Really pissed. He was also sincere. He said, gently, "Jack was my friend, and he had problems." Then he turned his back on me. I immediately got the feeling that I was no longer likely to be awoken by the messiah on redemption day. I'd pissed off the man who'd written: "The world is holy! The soul is holy! The skin is holy! The nose is holy! The tongue and cock and hand and asshole holy! / Everything is holy! everybody's holy! everywhere is holy! everyday is in eternity! Everyman's an angel!"

Delmore Schwartz is another American artist. I came across his poetry and stories around the same time that I discovered Lou Reed, and I had no idea that Reed studied with Schwartz. When I found out, I felt like I'd been let into a conspiracy—not the Jews-own-the-media kind of conspiracy, but the fantasy that a queer Jewish kid with no friends pieces together in his bedroom while listening to LPs, reading poetry, and making connections. Schwartz crested at twenty-four with the beautiful, devastating story "In Dreams Begin Responsibilities," which is about the narrator watching a movie that shows his parents' courtship. The story, written in 1935, takes place in 1909, before the war, before the Depression, and it's full of foreboding. Toward the end, he stands up in the theater and shouts at the screen: "Don't do it. It's not too late to change your minds, both of you. Nothing good will come of it, only remorse, hatred, scandal, and two children whose characters are monstrous."

To me, that's the vision of America—of American history and of the prospects for the future—from the perspective of Jewish Romanticism as carried over from Germany, reality-checked in Brooklyn, and translated from Yiddish.

Who else? Carole King will go down in history as one of the great American songwriters: "(You Make Me Feel Like) a Natural Woman," "Will You Love Me Tomorrow," "One Fine Day." She's right up there with—

[*Audience member speaks.*]

Robert Zimmerman!

[*Bordowitz replies.*]

Yeah, Bob Dylan.

[*Another audience member speaks.*]

Burt Bacharach!

[*Bordowitz replies.*]

All right, all right—Barbra Streisand!

[*Laughter, chants of "Barbra, Barbra, Barbra!."*]

Who else? Jonathan Richman, of the Modern Lovers. He celebrated American themes; he understood rock and roll as the cornerstone of the culture. Lou Reed was proud of being an American artist: before the

Velvet Underground, he worked as a songwriter for Pickwick Records, which churned out copies of whatever music was hot at the moment. After studying with Schwartz, Reed got his chops by writing in every American idiom and copying every popular style—surf, soul, garage rock, and so on.

These artists believed in the promise of America. Allen Ginsberg believed in the promise of America. "America I'm putting my queer shoulder to the wheel"—you have to believe to write that line. Same goes for Abbie Hoffman, who was the son of Jewish immigrants, a patriot, a fan of American-flag shirts, a chief supporter of the 1968 candidacy of a pig—Pigasus—for president. They all had faith in the opportunity that was on offer in America, and unimaginable in the countries that their parents and grandparents had fled.

Opportunity, though, comes in limited supply. Trauma follows trauma—at least in *my* experience. And that's how you get Jewish humor: the endless cycle of belief and disappointment, hope and despair. Jewish humor emerges as a response to the cruelty of the world, and often manifests as cruelty.

I grew up in a cruel household, which is to say a hilarious household: a household where, psychologically, we needed humor in order to survive.

My grandmother—my mother's mother, Gloria Glassman—was great; she called me *Greggles* or *Greggela*, and she could cut me down to size in a second. She was as cruel as *der teufel*, and she had the timing of Joan Rivers. I'd pose a question or ask for something, and she'd say: "*Hak mir nisht keyn tshaynik*!" Stop rattling my tea kettle! Or: "*Gay kocken offen yom*." Which means, "Go take a shit in the ocean." Whether you have to take a shit or not.

That's the kind of humor I understand. My grandmother gave me a template for my act, and also a motivation: I've been in therapy for years and years, I've spent thousands and thousands of dollars. How else am I going to redeem that investment?

My grandmother's favorite thing to say to me, from a very young age, was, "*Kish mir tuchus* in Macy's window." She used to say this five, six, ten times a day. "Kiss my ass in Macy's window." Basically, she was telling me to perform a humiliating sexual act on her in the most prominent display window in the most popular department store in New York City. What kind of thing is that to say to a kid?

Between telling me to go take a shit in the ocean and to perform humiliating sex acts on her, my grandmother was very kind, affectionate, and supportive. She loved me, really! If she hadn't, I wouldn't be able to do this right now. Who knows where I'd be? My dad left when I was four and, for a while, my mother wasn't around much, so my grandmother took care of me. I really annoyed her, but I also appreciated her. She must've been good enough, as D. W. Winnicott says. What I got was good enough.

My grandmother was key to my masculinity training. She worked at Mays, the department store, on Union Turnpike; she ruled the handbag section. At work, she'd wear a blouse and clip-on earrings. But at home, she'd wear housecoats covered in flowers, hair rollers as big as thermoses, and ... clip-on earrings. She never took them off.

My grandmother taught me how to shop. I loved going with her from department to department; I knew all the ladies at Mays. But my grandmother also taught me how to be tough. She smoked Pall Malls and drank Old Milwaukee out of the bottle. She cursed like a truck driver. She taught me most of my Yiddish curses. (In fact, my Yiddish mostly consists of curses.)

My stepfather was extremely cruel, which is to say that he was extremely funny. He had a classic routine, which he began when I was eight or so—a couple years after he married my mom. I'd be sitting on the carpet, watching TV, and my stepfather would be sitting on the couch behind me. He'd say to my mother: "Linda, do we have a son with a glass head? I'm just asking. Do we have a son with a glass head? Because I'm not seeing the TV right now."

Later, as a young Marxist living in Manhattan, I fell in love with Black Flag's "TV Party." Every night at the Bordowitz household had been a TV party and, as much as anything, that'd made me feel American. I was as brainwashed by the mass-media machine as every other kid! At the same time, I was made to resent the fact that we'd failed to improve our socioeconomic position. And, as I grew up, I became more and more alienated by the pap that we, the cretins of Kew Gardens, were consuming. I worked hard to get out of that place, to get out of that culture. Somehow, though, I'm still eating takeout on my hotel bed and watching *Seinfeld*; I'm still hearing "TV Party" in my head as the hours pass.

I guess I'm still the same kid from Queens—and the same Jew-pinko-queer. The irony!

TV party tonight
TV party tonight
TV party tonight
TV party tonight!

We're gonna have a TV party tonight
All right!
We're gonna have a TV party, all right
Tonight!

We've got nothing better to do
Than watch TV and have a couple of brews

Everybody's gonna hang out here tonight
All right!
We'll pass out on the couch, all right
Tonight!

We've got nothing better to do
Than watch TV and have a couple of brews

Don't talk about anything else
We don't want to know
We're dedicated to our favorite shows

That's Incredible!
Hill Street Blues!
Dallas!
Fridays!

We sit glued to the TV set all night
And every night
Why go into the outside world at all
It's such a fright

We've got nothing better to do
Than watch TV and have a couple of brews

TV news shows
What it's like out there
It's a scare
You can go out if you want
We wouldn't dare

We've got nothing better to do
Than watch TV and have a couple of brews

Don't talk about anything else

We don't want to know
We're dedicated to our favorite shows

My stepfather had another joke, which might help to explain why I became an artist: I used to make swirls of ketchup on my hamburgers, which took a long time. We didn't have the new ketchup technology: you flip the plastic bottle upside down, squeeze, and the pressure pushes the ketchup out! In the age before that landmark in the advance of consumer products, we made do with glass bottles. I had to focus in order to get the proper swirl, the right ketchup-to-beef ratio.

"Hey, Picasso! Picasso, are you done with the ketchup?" my stepfather said. "He's an artist, look!"

I tried not to let him break my concentration as I coaxed the ketchup out of the bottle, gradually circling from the perimeter to the center of the patty.

"Look at that hamburger!" he said with mock enthusiasm. "Behold the master at work."

I loved my mother, but she was not a good cook. I often didn't like what was being served, but I couldn't identify the reason. I'd just say, for instance, "The onions are giving me a headache." At which point, those of you who are parents would probably say, "Oh, Gregg, do you want a Tofurky dog? Do you want almond butter and artisanal jelly?" The goal, I'm told, is to get food into the child. But my stepfather took a different tack. He said, "Silver Moon Diner is open." If I didn't want to eat what my mother had cooked, I could walk down the street to the diner and buy myself a meal.

I never took him up on the offer: the Silver Moon was not welcoming to unaccompanied ten-year-olds.

Maybe I should have had more rachmones—sympathy—for my mother, who, every Sunday, made six meals and put them in the freezer, because she worked, too. And my stepfather wasn't going to cook. So we had frozen meals every night of the week, except on Saturday: dairy night! That could mean anything—anything you could do with eggs and milk. My mother's specialty, which I make to this day when I'm really feeling depressed, was spaghetti with ... *American sauce*: melted margarine and ketchup.

How American can you get?!?

I'll memorialize my mother with a song that precedes "We're a Happy Family" in the canon of Jewish family portraits: Sophie Tucker, a star of Yiddish theater in New York in the 1920s, singing "My Yiddishe Momme"—an ode to self sacrificing immigrant parents that somehow became an international hit in the years leading up to World War II.

Of things I should be thankful for I've had a goodly share
And as I sit here in the comfort of my cozy chair
My fancy takes me to a humble east side tenement
Three flights up in the rear to where my childhood
    days were spent
It wasn't much like paradise but amid the dirt and all
There sat the sweetest angel, one that I fondly call

My Yiddishe momme, I need her more than ever now
My Yiddishe momme, I'd like to kiss that wrinkled brow
I long to hold her hands once more as in days gone by
And ask her to forgive me for things I did that
    made her cry
How few were her pleasures, she never cared for
    fashion's styles
Her jewels and treasures, she found them in her
    baby's smiles
Oh, I know that I owe what I am today
To that dear little lady so old and gray
To that wonderful Yiddishe momme of mine

I loved my mother, and I miss her, but we had a tough relationship. After I was diagnosed with AIDS, well—I used to be really fat when I was a kid. You know, I got rewarded for eating, and not for much else. For my bar mitzvah, I wore a three-piece husky-size polyester herringbone suit, and I looked like a sofa. When I got sick, I lost a ton of weight. It's called lipodystrophy: the amount of fat tissue in your body decreases, and sometimes the fat migrates to odd places. For a long time, I avoided going home because I looked so bad. Finally, in

1997, my sister got married, so I went to visit my family where the diaspora ends: Florida.

I'd come out to my family a long time before, and I'd told them that I'd gotten HIV, but no one had said anything to my grandparents. I couldn't have that conversation with them. At the time, as activists, we were cool with not telling our families. We were like, "You take on what you can handle, as you can handle it." So I greeted my grandmother right before the wedding, and I was emaciated, my face was drained of color.

She went nuts. She couldn't stop screaming.

[*Flaps arms, shrieks at a high pitch.*]

"My grandson has AIDS! My grandson has AIDS! You have AIDS! You didn't tell us?!? My grandson has AIDS!"

I was with my partner at the time, who told my grandmother, "Calm down. He's all right. He's taking the pills and they're working."

She kept screaming, "My grandson has AIDS! My grandson has AIDS!"

Everyone was looking at us. Later, after the wedding, I was helping my mother prepare for dinner, spreading the tablecloth, and she said, "Why didn't you tell me?"

"What?" I said.

"Why didn't you tell me you look like this? So I could, you know—warn people."

That hurt. She didn't ask why I hadn't told them that AIDS was ravaging my body, that I wasn't only infected but *sick*. She said, "Why didn't you tell us that you look like this, so that we could manage the situation?"

I've been living with AIDS for thirty years—more than half of my life. I'm lucky enough to have survived until 1996, when protease inhibitors were introduced, and to have gotten access to those life-saving drugs, which are still keeping me—and a minority of people with the disease—alive. To *still* have AIDS and *still* be alive is a cosmic joke.

Next time, I'm going to begin the show with that joke. There's nowhere to go from there but up, right?

The AIDS crisis is not over; it's still beginning. History will regard our era as the early days of the AIDS crisis, when the fortunate few stood on stages and made jokes while forty thousand Americans were infected and sixteen thousand died, the vast majority of them Black and Latinx; while two million people around the world were infected and one million died; while only half of the thirty-seven million people living with AIDS were on life-saving drugs.

Is there anyone else in the audience who's living with HIV? We used to do this at meetings of activists in order to recognize that the people with HIV were always among us, the speaker wasn't the only one. You don't have to say anything; I don't mean to make any of you feel vulnerable. But raise your hand if you'd like to—if you're living with HIV.

[*Several audience members raise their hands.*]

Thank you.

After 1996, my friends and I took a while to wrap our minds around the fact that we weren't about to die; suddenly, we had more life, maybe years, maybe decades. I've never really been able to accept that I'll keep on living after so many have died. I don't know what it means to be a survivor. I didn't do anything that caused me to be on this stage today; I didn't do anything that my friends didn't do. I had access to medical care and, eventually, protease inhibitors, because the effect of the virus on me was relatively slow and limited. I'm alive because of privilege and luck.

Someone once asked me if, having survived until 1996 and received lifesaving drugs, I could accept that I'd have a normal lifespan. *A normal lifespan*. That idea is egregious, right? What's a normal lifespan? There's no such thing. The only response I could muster was, "Well, with any luck I won't live much longer!"

It's OK—I'm talking to my therapist. And fortunately, I don't experience stigma as a survivor. But I do experience pain. People in my generation went through some very difficult times in the '80s and '90s. We even made up horrible clichés to describe what happened: "I lost half my address book." "Some of my best friends are quilts." And the pain that we went through—that's what seems to be missing from the histories of the AIDS crisis so far.

Essex Hemphill, a writer and friend who died from AIDS in 1995, articulated that pain in the poem "Cordon Negro," from 1985. I miss him, and I'm pained by the fact that he isn't more well known, so I read from his work whenever I can.

> I drink champagne early in the morning
> instead of leaving my house
> with an M16 and nowhere to go.
>
> I'm dying twice as fast
> as any other American
> between eighteen and thirty-five.
> This disturbs me,
> but I try not to show it in public.
>
> Each morning I open my eyes is a miracle.
> The blessing of opening them
> is temporary on any given day.
>
> I could be taken out,
> I could go off,
> I could forget to be careful.

Even my brothers, hunted, hunt me.
I am the only one who values my life
and sometimes I don't give a damn.

My love life can kill me.
I'm faced daily with choosing violence
or a demeanor that saves every other life
but my own.

I won't cross-over.
It's time someone else came to me
not to patronize me physically,
sexually, or humorously.

I'm sick of being an endangered species,
sick of being a goddamn statistic.
So what are my choices?

I could leave with no intention
of coming home tonight,
go crazy downtown and raise hell
on a rooftop with my rifle.
I could live for a brief moment
on the six o'clock news,
or masquerade another day
through the corridors of commerce
and American dreams.

I'm dying twice as fast
as any other American.
So I pour myself a glass of champagne,
I cut it with a drop of orange juice.

After I swallow my liquid valium,
my private celebration
for being alive

this morning,
I leave my shelter,
I guard my life with no apologies.
My concerns are small
and personal.

As you know by now, my sense of humor is rooted in my anger, and in my experience of alienation, injustice, and death. I don't believe in humor as palliative, much less curative. I believe in humor as a vessel for angst, resentment, frustration, and outrage. I believe in humor as a force that binds together those of us who are angsty, resentful, frustrated, and outraged.

Look at me: you think I'm going to be cured when I get off the stage? I'm already looking to the post-show depression. My routine is a smorgasbord that leads to the post-show depression, the greenroom shame spiral. Yet I find myself on stage quite often. Why? Humor may not help, not immediately. But, as with an infused gummy, the effects, when you finally feel them, can be extraordinary and long-lasting. Beware!

Twenty years ago, I heard Sarah Silverman tell a joke about AIDS that really got to me, that's still working its way through my system. Silverman is one of the few Jewish comedians whose focus on identity goes beyond jokes about Jewfros and neurosis, and actually deals with the performance of ethnicity, gender, and nationality. In the routine, she talks about her niece's school barring her from playing tag, for fear of damaging her self-esteem, and about the importance of motivating kids to win.

> I tell my niece that every time she loses at tag, an angel gets AIDS. ... I tell her that a beautiful angel gets full-blown AIDS. And, you know what, she wins! So think about that. I tell her that when God gives you AIDS—and God *does* give you AIDS, by the way—make lemon-AIDS. It's called positive spin. That's what we should steal from corporate America, you know? ... The whole idea of taking something terrible, something tragic, and spinning it into something good. If American Airlines were smart, their slogan would be: "American Airlines: first through the towers." Because it is something in which they came first, right?

For Silverman to make a joke about AIDS was really brave. She's all about playing to type: she presents herself as a naive Jewish American Princess, which works because she's so conventionally beautiful. The premise of her act is that the words are just falling out of her mouth; she can't believe what she's saying. And the joke is terrible! The point is to violate a taboo, but also to demonstrate that there's no such thing as a good joke about AIDS. I find the routine to be really empathetic, in part because the delivery is devoid of empathy: Silverman has to be on the inside—she has to be talking to people who understand AIDS, people who have AIDS—in order to do the act as if she's on the outside.

The first time I was ever publicly addressed—and not shamed—as a person with AIDS was in 1996, when I saw an ad for the drug I was taking on a Chicago subway platform. The ad showed a mountain climber with bursting biceps gripping the face of a rock. Could antiretrovirals turn me into that blonde sportsman? For more than a decade, people like me had been excluded from society, banished from view. We were thought of as a mass of infectious outsiders who threatened public health. When we were interviewed on television, we were shown as scrambled faces next to potted palms. Only a few people—Max Navarre and Michael Callen, for instance—were willing to have their faces appear on television. My cohort of activists took our cues from them: we had enough privilege to take the risk of going public about having HIV.

Suddenly, with the introduction of retroviral drugs, we were welcomed back into the fold. The AIDS crisis was over! In reality, though, the AIDS crisis is still beginning. Why? AIDS touched—and continues to touch—every other issue: homelessness, racism, drug use, economic inequality, health care, the position of women in society, and so on. Those of us who were working with ACT UP in the late '80s weren't involved in a single-issue movement. We thought we were part of a revolution!

ACT UP was split between people who wanted to get drugs into bodies and people who wanted to get socialized medicine for the country; I was split, too, because I wanted to get drugs into *my* body, but I really thought the movement had the potential to get socialized medicine for the country. And, well, I eat contradictions for lunch: I fought for both, never mind the debate. Why choose? Why not get drugs into bodies in order to get health care for all?

Unfortunately, we still aren't getting drugs into every body that needs them, and we still don't have health care for all. Researchers are working on a vaccine to prevent people from getting AIDS, but they're not really working on a cure. Researchers aren't interested in me. They're not trying to save the survivors. And that's fine; I understand. Yet I can't help but think that, in two hundred years, if we survive ecological collapse and mass extinction, if there are such things as humanity and history, we'll look back and say: the AIDS crisis was still beginning. There were thirty-six million people on the planet with HIV, and only half of them had access to lifesaving drugs.

The accounts of AIDS in books and films cause me a great deal of pain. Even sophisticated documentaries like *How to Survive a Plague*—in which I appear—suggest that we're looking back on a crisis that's over. And that's more than I can say for hagiographies and Hollywood fables like *Philadelphia*. They tend to depict AIDS as a disease that afflicts gay white men, who often happen to be handsome, charismatic, and affluent. They don't tell the story of AIDS that I experienced, and they don't speak to the fact that so few people have access to the drugs that are keeping me alive. They don't treat AIDS as an ongoing pandemic. They don't mention the alarming rate of HIV infection among people of color in this country. They present AIDS as *history*.

Well, if you think the crisis ended with people like me being lucky enough to get pills and survive, you're wrong. If you think that most people who are getting or living with HIV are going to be lucky enough to survive, you're wrong. HIV is the leading killer of women in the world. The majority of women who are dying from HIV are people of color in the Global South, mostly in sub-Saharan Africa. And the funding for international AIDS prevention and treatment has collapsed.

The divide between the Global North and the Global South reflects the divide in the United States between the North and South: a disproportionate number of Americans who are infected with HIV each year live in the South. And, again, half the people in the world who need drugs can't get them, or they don't have access to clean water, so the drugs—the drugs alone—are useless. We're dealing with a raging pandemic, and we're still at the beginning.

Are you waiting for the punch line?

I realized when I got on stage that I forgot to take my pills this morning. That's what you're getting. I know, I know—not now, not here! Fortunately, a trained professional—my therapist—is in attendance; we'll be speaking about this in the coming days, at great cost to me. I don't need to talk about my anger, disbelief, and guilt with all of you, right?

That's what you get to do as a comedian, though: you trade on your pain. That's what Lenny Bruce did, that's what Richard Pryor did. Bruce read from the transcripts of his obscenity trials and talked about the psychological toll of being harassed by the police, bankrupted by the courts, and blacklisted by clubs. Pryor mined the most awful experiences of addiction and racism for material. He had enormous pathos, and he was honest about the transaction between himself and the audience: he was turning his pain into currency.

That's what you get to do as an AIDS artist, too. My inbox explodes every November, a week or two before World AIDS Day, with emails from people who're looking for speakers. I'm the AIDS artist—the surviving AIDS artist—so I get to represent everyone else, everyone who died. "You knew Frank Moore, right? Tell us about him." "What was David Wojnarowicz like?"

On the one hand: how can I say woe is me? I'm alive. On the other hand: woe is me. It's been a tough life.

The obligation to represent others—and the expectation that I'll trade on my pain—has followed me for thirty years, since I decided to make my life into my material. I try to believe in myself as an artist and not a poster boy, and I try to expand my idiom, my repertoire. Fortunately, as my therapist will attest, I'm a postmodern person: I wear identities like hats. But identities have genuine consequences in the world. You can get killed for your identity. Your life is at stake when you're stigmatized.

Want a shortcut? Read Erving Goffman's *Stigma*, from 1963. I'll boil it down for you: Goffman treats stigma with a tremendous amount of latitude. He talks about the types of stigma that all kinds of people face, because of sexuality, race, ethnicity, ability, drug addiction, incarceration—they add up and add up. Finally, he comes to the conclusion that the only unimpeachable identity in the United States in 1963 is a white male who's married to a woman, has children, and is good at sports. The only one!

Goffman is brilliant because he understands code-switching. *Stigma* is the original study of code-switching. Goffman understands how and why people move between identities, how each stigmatized identity creates an inside and outside: if you're an outsider or outlier, you go to places where you're no longer an outsider or outlier. You go to places like this—where you can be ... legendary. Or aspire to be.

I'm OK: *I'll get there.*

What am I trying to say? I believe that an army of the sick cannot be defeated.

How do you resist fascism? An army of the sick. How do you put an end to a pandemic? An army of the sick.

I believe that, if we take all the stigmas in the room, and if we all identify at the level of those stigmas, then we have a chance. I believe in the Ramones's "Cretin Hop."

> There's no stoppin' the cretins from hoppin'
> You gotta keep it beatin' for all the hoppin' cretins
>
> Cretin, cretin
> I'm gonna go for a whirl with my cretin girl

My feet won't stop doin' the Cretin Hop
Cretin, cretin

One-two-three-four, cretins want to hop some more
Four-five-six-seven, all good cretins go to heaven

There's no stoppin' the cretins from hoppin'
You gotta keep it beatin' for all the hoppin' cretins

Cretin, cretin
I'm gonna go for a whirl with my cretin girl
My feet won't stop doin' the Cretin Hop
Cretin, cretin

One, two, three, four, cretins want to hop some more
Four, five, six, seven, all good cretins go to heaven

Do the cretins understand themselves to be cretins? Only when they leave the world of cretins, right? Only when they cross an ocean, border, or suspension bridge. My grandfather was born in Bessarabia, in a shtetl that's now part of Ukraine, where his family lived for who-knows-how-many generations. They were part of the second wave of Jewish immigrants, who fled the pogroms in Eastern Europe long before the Nazis came to power. I learned a lot about masculinity from my grandfather. I don't know where I'd be—or where my act would be—without his hard-earned pessimism, which, in my opinion, is the perfect complement to my grandmother's manic depression and unrelenting cruelty. But you be the judge.

I learned more and more about masculinity from my grandfather as I came to understand who he was outside of our family, our neighborhood, our community. After I moved from Long Island to Manhattan when I was eighteen, I used to meet my grandfather at the loading dock of the clock factory in Flatiron. One day, I walked up to the group of men gathered at the loading dock and I saw somebody who, from behind, looked like my grandfather, but he was speaking Spanish. When he turned around, I realized he *was* my grandfather—and that I'd never known he spoke Spanish, which made perfect sense given that his entire crew was from Latin America. I was happy to see him—we loved each other very much—and I surprised him by planting a big kiss on his lips.

In my world, in my childhood, men greeted each other by kissing on the lips. I used to love how they kissed at family parties, how they lined up to hold each other's shoulders, whisper into each other's ears, and peck each other on the lips. They did this with great tenderness, intimacy, and a casual sense of ceremony. By the time I was a teenager, though, I knew not to kiss men on the lips at other families' houses. But somehow I hadn't quite absorbed the larger lesson; I hadn't realized that the norms of my Jewish enclave didn't apply elsewhere. And might very well be misunderstood!

So ... I locked lips with my grandfather, right in front of all the guys on his crew. And they had no idea what to do. They weren't just speechless, they were turned into statues. They had no idea who I was! I didn't necessarily look like my grandfather's grandson: my mother gave birth to me when she was eighteen, so I could have been a younger ... friend? Disciple? My grandfather didn't make a scene. But he corrected me: "That's not what men do."

Only after I started to identify as queer did I experience men kissing like this again. When I was in the AIDS movement, we greeted each other by kissing on the lips. We wanted to combat homophobia and, importantly, prove to ourselves that there was no reason to fear infection through kissing.

I kept going to see my grandfather in Flatiron, and I tried to keep our lives from drifting too far apart. I realized that I was, inexorably, moving away from him, away from his experience of the world, away from the world that he'd wanted for me. At the same time, I wanted to believe that my path would always loop back and intersect with his, that I would never be lost to him and he would never be lost to me. We could find a way to share the past in the present and the present in the future, I thought.

What does that mean? I took him out for sushi. Sushi: the past in the present and the present in the future. Messianic lunchtime.

I came from Queens, remember: we didn't eat a lot of things, and sushi was one of them. Like a lot of people, I fell in love with sushi in the early '80s, and I wanted to convert my grandfather. One day, on our way to sushi, we walked down the street, passing the Flatiron Building, and I saw a handsome man in his late twenties. To me, at the time, he seemed like an older man. We clocked each other—we looked each other in the eyes, swiveling our heads slightly as we got closer. He smiled. I smiled. And then I passed him.

My grandfather was quiet for about ten feet. Then he said, "Did you know that guy?"

"No, he just smiled at me and I smiled back," I said.

My grandfather shook his head.

"What's wrong with smiling?" I asked.

We took a few more steps. Then my grandfather stopped and turned to me. He had a grave look on his face. "Only idiots smile," he said.

[*Applause.*]

Acknowledgments

We are not alone in our thoughts and reflections, even in our most private moments. Thinking out loud—which is what I do when I perform—requires many imagined, virtual, epistolary, and face-to-face conversations. They span a lifetime; they are my greatest source of inspiration and ideas. I am grateful to everyone with whom I've had such conversations. (If, through some lapse, I've neglected to mention anyone, please forgive me.) Some people may be surprised to find themselves on this list, but one never knows the influence one might have. I thank the following people for supporting or inspiring these monologues: Ortez Alderson (z"l), Stephen Andrews, Sam Avrett, Ari Banias, David Barr, Morgan Bassichis, Lauren Berlant (z"l), Maya Binyam, Margaret Black, Johanna Burton, Jean Carlomusto, Leidy Churchman, Ron Clark, Douglas Crimp (z"l), Ann Cvetkovich, Moyra Davey, Susanne Desroches, Rosalyn Deutsche, Mark Dion, D. Denenge Duyst-Akpem, Peter Eeley, Anthony Elms, Richard Elovich, Joy Episalla, Steve Fagin, Robyn Farrell, Corrine Fitzpatrick, Jonathan Flately, Andrea Fraser, Ann Goldstein, John Greyson, Joseph Grigely, Rabbi Miriam Grossman, Cat Gund, Liza Johnson, Rashid Johnson, Arnold Kemp, Molly Kleiman, Alhena Katsof, Zoe Leonard, Glenn

Ligon, Rabbi Ellen Lippmann, Josiah McElheny, Benny Merris, James Meyer, Lara Mimosa Montes, Helen Molesworth, Fred Moten, Ulrike Müller, Eileen Myles, Ray Navarro (z"l), Solveig Nelson, Sara O'Keefe, Craig Owens (z"l), Claire Pentecost, Perel, Alexander Provan, Yvonne Rainer, Susanne Sachsse, Sarah Schulman, Cantor Lisa B. Segal, Marc Seigel, Amy Sillman, Jason Simon, Pamela Sneed, Stephanie Snyder, Kendall Thomas, Lynne Tillman, Wu Tsang, Anthony Viti, Christopher Williams, Daniel Wolfe, Carrie Yamaoka, and Molly Zuckerman-Hartung.

My mother, Linda Bordowitz (z"l), was very funny and smart. She loved bad puns. She had a great record collection. Her taste in music defined mine. She taught me how to dance. My stepfather, Martin Bordowitz (z"l), provided my childhood homes with excellent stereo equipment and sample albums culled from the KLH speaker factory where he worked. My sister, Traci Cronk, is hilarious. Max Glassman (z"l), my maternal grandfather, gave me my love for Judaism, my knowledge of religious observance, and an appropriately pessimistic outlook on life. My maternal grandmother, Gloria Glassman (z"l), was also an influential pessimist who had the timing (and loving cruelty) of the best comedians.

My partner, Kristine Woods, is my constant interlocutor, and I am deeply grateful for her support. Kristine converses with me (and listens to my playlists) on a daily basis, from the moment we wake up through meals, walks, and errands, until we go to sleep. She gives me some of my best ideas.

—*Gregg Bordowitz*

Hechsher

On the day I received the letter accepting me to rabbinical school, I had a dream in which I grew a long white beard. From that day on, I understood gender and the rabbinate as both tools and weapons—and as an opening. And I determined that I—a woman, a lesbian, a questioner—would always maintain that opening.

Gregg Bordowitz appeared in my life as a participant in—and then a member of—Kolot Chayeinu, the nontraditional community I founded in 1993 and served as rabbi for twenty-five years. Gregg saw Kolot Chayeinu as the spiritual home that he needed when he joined, in 1997, and he has gone on to help make the community into the home that others have needed (even if they haven't known as much). He regularly participates in and leads weekly Torah study sessions, to which he brings his own —often queer— take on the Torah portion. And he has drawn a host of fellow artists, Jewish and not, who come to learn, argue, and derive meaning from the Torah—the best results of studying the Torah. Unlike some people in this weekly conversation with beings divine and human, he also stays for the Shabbat prayer service, as his forebears did— and as they never did.

I first encountered Gregg as a friend of a friend; both were linked to the late great Allen Ginsberg.

I am a poetry lover, and I was working at the 14th Street Y in Manhattan when I was, astonishingly, asked to lead a Jewish funeral for Ginsberg. For his family, the large, communal, Buddhist memorial had not been enough. So, in the pouring rain, I trooped to a backwater cemetery in New Jersey with Ginsberg's family, adherents, and fellow artists, including Gregg, to bury the "poet of his generation," to use the words that the late Rabbi Zalman Schachter-Shalomi suggested for his gravestone.

Ginsberg had his own questions (and made his own decisions) about his gender, as Schachter-Shalomi surely did, and as I do. Now, thanks to Gregg—a gift of a Jewish queer man—readers will get to ask themselves such questions; we will all get to question and rethink our styles of masculinity (and femininity) as we go about our days in this wildly uncertain world.

—Rabbi Ellen Lippmann

A *hechsher* commonly refers to the certification by a rabbi or *kashrut* authority that a food or beverage product is kosher. Books of Jewish scholarship also feature a hechsher, which authorizes and blesses the work. For *Some Styles of Masculinity*, Gregg Bordowitz requested a hechsher from Rabbi Ellen Lippmann, the founder and Rabbi Emerita of his Brooklyn congregation, Kolot Chayeinu (Voices of Our Lives). Lippmann also serves on the boards of Jews for Racial & Economic Justice and IntegrateNYC, and she is a mentor with the Clergy Leadership Incubator and Taproot programs. She is the founder and co-chair of CAMMEERR, a multiracial, cross-faith group of leaders working to "cross the divides that limit our work together and harm our people."

Triple Canopy is a magazine based in New York City. Triple Canopy publishes and presents work by artists, writers, and researchers, primarily through the magazine's digital platform but also in books, conversations, and performances, among other media and experiences. Founded in 2007, Triple Canopy is a nonprofit 501(c)(3) organization.

Support for *Some Styles of Masculinity* has been provided by the Stolbun Family, Gregory R. Miller and Michael Wiener, and the Douglas F. Cooley Memorial Art Gallery at Reed College. Triple Canopy is grateful to them and to the generous supporters of the magazine's 2020 benefit, which honored Gregg Bordowitz, as well as Leidy Churchman, Rashid Johnson, Amy Sillman, and Christopher Williams, who contributed artworks. Triple Canopy also thanks the New Museum, the Art Institute of Chicago, and MoMA PS1, where Bordowitz has performed *Some Styles of Masculinity*.

Triple Canopy gratefully acknowledges the generous support of the Andy Warhol Foundation for the Visual Arts, the Horace W. Goldsmith Foundation, Lambent Foundation Fund of Tides Foundation, the National Endowment for the Arts, the New York State Council on the Arts, the New York City Department of Cultural Affairs in partnership with the City Council, and the Opaline Fund, as well the magazine's Board of Directors, Director's Circle, Publishers Circle, and the many individuals whose contributions sustain the magazine. Triple Canopy also receives support from the Henry Luce Foundation, the Willem de Kooning Foundation, and the Teiger Foundation through the Coalition of Small Arts New York.

Also by Gregg Bordowitz

Glenn Ligon: Untitled (I Am a Man) (Afterall Books, 2018)

General Idea: Imagevirus (Afterall Books, 2010)

Volition (Printed Matter and Badlands Unlimited, 2009)

The AIDS Crisis Is Ridiculous and Other Writings, 1986–2003 (MIT Press, 2004)

Also Published by Triple Canopy

International Art English, by Alix Rule and David Levine with Mariam Ghani and Alexander Provan (ebook, 2018)

Andy Warhol: The Series, by Hilton Als with Jennifer Krasinski (2017)

The Amme Talks, by Ulf Stolterfoht, translated by Shane Anderson; with an afterword by Peter Dittmer, translated by Megan Ewing (2017)

S as in Samsam, by Sowon Kwon (Triple Canopy and Secretary Press, 2017)

Not Dead But Sleeping, by Anna Della Subin (2017)

On Value, edited by Triple Canopy and Ralph Lemon, with contributions by Kevin Beasley, Claire Bishop, Philip Bither, Paula Court, Adrienne Edwards, Tom Finkelpearl, Ana Janevski, Claudia La Rocco, Thomas J. Lax, Ralph Lemon, Glenn Ligon, Glenn Lowry, Sarah Michelson, Fred Moten, Adam Pendleton, Yvonne Rainer, Will Rawls, David Velasco, and Nari Ward (2015)

Speculations ("The future is ______"), edited by Triple Canopy, with contributions by Fatima Al Qadiri, David Auerbach, Gopal Balakrishnan, Ray Brassier, Holly Jean Buck, Ted Chiang, Jace Clayton, CA Conrad, John Crowley, Samuel Delany, Esther Dyson, Silvia Federici, Rivka Galchen, David Graeber, N. Katherine Hayles, Katie Kitamura, Josh Kline, Benjamin Kunkel, Rachel Kushner, Lynn Hershman Leeson, Mary Mattingly, Naeem Mohaiemen, Evgeny Morozov, Hương Ngô, Trevor Paglen, Ashwin Parameswaran, Christian Parenti, Laura Poitras, Srikanth Reddy, David Rieff, Kim Stanley Robinson, Norman Rush, Sukhdev Sandhu, Edward Snowden, Astra Taylor, Mierle Laderman Ukeles, and Kathi Weeks (2015)

Headless, by K. D. with Alexander Provan (Triple Canopy and Sternberg Press, 2015)

Corrected Slogans: Reading and Writing Conceptualism, edited by Triple Canopy, with contributions by Nora Abrams, Andrea Andersson, Erica Baum, Franklin Bruno, Corina Copp, Michael Corris, Brian Droitcour, Jim Fletcher, Zachary German, Lucy Ives, Aaron Kunin, Margaret Lee, Paul Legault, K. Silem Mohammad, Ken Okiishi, R. H. Quaytman, Katie Raissian, Ariana Reines, William S. Smith, Mónica de la Torre, Gretchen Wagner, Hannah Whitaker, and Matvei Yankelevich (Triple Canopy and MCA Denver, 2013)

The Binder and the Server, by Triple Canopy and Colby Chamberlain (2012)

Gregg Bordowitz is an artist, writer, activist, and educator who lives in New York City. He is the author of *The AIDS Crisis Is Ridiculous and Other Writings, 1986–2003* (2004), *Volition* (2009), *General Idea: Imagevirus* (2010), and *Glenn Ligon: Untitled (I Am a Man)* (2018). Bordowitz's work has been exhibited at Artists Space, the Solomon R. Guggenheim Museum, the Museum of Modern Art, the New Museum, and the Whitney Museum, among other institutions. His retrospective, "Gregg Bordowitz: I Wanna Be Well," was organized by the Douglas F. Cooley Memorial Art Gallery, Reed College (Portland), and subsequently presented at the Art Institute of Chicago and MoMA PS1 (New York). Bordowitz has made numerous contributions to Triple Canopy, including the three-episode advice show *Answers with Questions*, and was honored at the magazine's 2020 benefit.

Hua Hsu is a writer living in New York City. He is a staff writer at the New Yorker and an associate professor of English and director of the American Studies program at Vassar College. Hsu has contributed to Artforum, the *Atlantic*, *Slate*, the *Wire*, and Triple Canopy, among other publications, and has been a fellow at the New York Public Library's Dorothy and Lewis B. Cullman Center and the New America Foundation. He is the author of *A Floating Chinaman: Fantasy and Failure Across the Pacific* (2016), as well as a forthcoming memoir, *Stay True*, and an essay collection, *Impostor Syndrome*.